Strategies of
Competition
in the Bank Card Business

Strategies of Competition

in the Bank Card Business

Innovation Management in a Complex Economic Environment

JARUNEE WONGLIMPIYARAT

sussex
ACADEMIC
PRESS

BRIGHTON • PORTLAND

2 4 6 8 10 9 7 5 3 1

First published in hardcover 2004, and in paperback 2005 in Great Britain by
SUSSEX ACADEMIC PRESS
PO Box 2950
Brighton BN2 5SP

and in the United States of America by
SUSSEX ACADEMIC PRESS
920 NE 58th Ave   Suite 300
Portland, Oregon 97213-3786

British Library Cataloguing in Publication Data
A CIP catalogue record for this book is available from the British Library.

Library of Congress Cataloging-in-Publication Data
Wonglimpiyarat, Jarunee.
    Strategies of competition in the bank card business : innovation management in a complex economic environment / Jarunee Wonglimpiyarat.
        p.   cm.
    Includes bibliographical references and index.
    ISBN 1-903900-55-7 (alk. pbk)
    1. Debit cards   2. Bank credit cards.   3. Smart cards.   I. Title.
HG1643 .W66   2003
332.7′6—dc21
                                                                    2003012805
                                                                    CIP

Typeset and designed by G&G Editorial, Brighton
Printed and bound in Great Britain by MPG Books Ltd, Bodmin, Cornwall
This book is printed on acid-free paper.

Contents

Preface   vi

Acknowledgements   ix

1 ATM/Cash Cards   1

2 Credit Cards   21

3 EFTPOS/Debit Cards   38

4 Competition, Innovation and Performance:
   The Evolution of the Bank Card Business   57

5 Smart Cards   76

Notes   114

References   118

Index   122

Preface

Innovations in financial services – specifically ATM/cash cards, credit cards, EFTPOS/debit cards and smart cards – have brought about major changes in the global banking and commercial sectors. This book traces the development of these innovations, examining their commercial and industry impact since their introduction.

Bank card innovations have initiated new strategies of competition in the US and UK banking sectors. In the UK banking sector (which is the main focus of the book), financial innovations development remains the most advanced anywhere in the world today. An examination of the UK market is accompanied by analysis of the smart card innovation, and a review of the latest developments in the field of electronic financial solutions. Competing innovations in smart card financial applications technology are placed in the context of potential possibilities for the future development and direction of the smart card.

Bankers, financial institution workers, postgraduate students

The ATM/cash card innovation is the development of an ATM (Automated Teller Machine) network using automated cash machines to dispense banking services to customers on the basis of a magnetic (swipe) card and a Personal Identification Number (PIN). An ATM network consists of data terminals linked to host processors by leased lines. ATMs replace the functions of tellers in receiving and dispensing cash, funds transfer between accounts, balance enquiries, etc. ATMs provide convenient services unrestricted by banking hours. The ATM type of service allows customers to have a quick, convenient way to access money in their accounts. All cards issued with the Visa Plus or MasterCard Cirrus logos can be used in any cash machine worldwide that displays those logos. The adoption of ATM technology in banking is intended to provide better access to cash, through extending the times at which cash withdrawals can be made, and improve efficiency in service delivery.

The **EFTPOS/debit card innovation** is the development of a card-based electronic payment system, which allows an instant payment directly debited from the customer's account by using debit cards. An EFTPOS system enables the customers to make payments securely since the card is linked to the customer's current account. The EFTPOS/debit card provides convenient services by directly debiting customers' accounts at the point of sale, avoiding the need to carry cash. Thus, the complexities of using the machine (terminal) are transferred to the service providers. Consumers can use EFTPOS services at both financial institutions and retailers.

and those involved in technology management studies are presented with a comprehensive history of the bank card, thus enabling new speculations and observations about the present and future states of the bank card industry.

The development of card innovations is accurately and thoroughly documented, demonstrating how new and advanced solutions to the problems posed by bank cards propelled this purchasing and transaction mode into becoming a driving force in the modern commerical/banking sectors. As the technology necessary to accommodate commercial card usage is easily obtainable from technology suppliers, innovators are constantly looking for specific strategies to improve business opportunities. Interviews have been conducted with industry leaders in the card business, and their ideas reflect the market-driven strategic viewpoint presented here. Case studies are linked in with challenging theories in technology management to provide arenas of debate in financial innovation and management.

Technology management and technology strategy often focus on innovation solutions as a simplified process towards commercialization. The integration of technology management with business strategies and its accompanying complications in the financial service industry is still, however, relatively unexplored territory. The essential uniqueness of managing financial innovations is emphasized here, including:

- Research on the theme of managing financial innovations for competitive advantage;
- The integration of technology with competitive strategies in order to formulate, evaluate and compare a range of strategic

options which are central to a successful innovation management policy;

- Flowcharts presenting the complete innovation process from development to commercialization, charting each stage of the evolution of financial solutions;
- Insights into the future of new bank card innovations – for example, smart cards and the strategic direction necessary to ensure a propserous future for the financial services industry.

The factual data presented is correct up to the end of 2002. The bank card industry in 2003 has yet to witness, at the time of going to press, any major developments that would affect the marketing strategies and competiton theories detailed herein. Indeed, 2003 has so far witnessed a gradual decline in economic growth and a subsequent market slowdown – far from ideal conditions in which to launch a new financial application. It is the 1990s dataset, however, which gives the broadest and most accurate document of the development of the bank card industry. There are two reasons for this. First, the 1990s saw the most radical overhauls in the banking card sector – the introduction of new technologies and the first integrations with other systems, such as the Internet, which resulted in Internet credit cards like the Marbles and Egg cards. Second, retrospective analysis allows an empiric examination of the dynamic factors involved in bank and smart card evolution.

The book is divided into five chapters. **Chapters 1, 2** and **3** trace the historical developments of ATM/cash cards, credit cards and debit cards, as well as analyzing the competitive strategies employed by the major industry players. These strategies are discussed in the context of the technical obstacles and difficulties of maximising potential benefits facing innovators. **Chapter 4** looks at the evolution of the bank card and the patterns that have emerged from its development in terms of innovation, competition and performance. And **chapter 5** analyzes the smart card innovation; going beyond simple definition of the uses and advantages of chip card technology, a detailed examination is presented of the various futures open to smart card innovators, all competing to launch an effective smart-card-for-financial-application platform.

Acknowledgements

There are a number of people I would like to express my gratitude to with these words of acknowledgement. Foremost, I appreciate the understanding and encouragement of my parents through their support in the writing of this book. I would like to express my gratitude to Professor Douglas Wood, who provided advice and professional support. I am indebted to Professor Denis Loveridge and Dr. Ketmanee Ausadamongkol, who assisted me with the conceptualisation of the research presented here. And I would like to thank Professor Tudor Rickards and Professor Steve Worthington for comments, criticism and advice.

Finally, I would like to convey my sincere gratitude to Mr. John Hardy (LINK Interchange Network) and Mr. Michael Lewis (APACS). The book's contents were greatly enhanced by their advice. Their professional help has assisted me in presenting a conceptual framework for managing financial innovations.

ATM/Cash Cards

The ATM/cash card innovation in this book is considered as the development of an ATM (Automated Teller Machine) network using automated cash machines to dispense banking services to customers on the basis of a magnetic (swipe) card and a Personal Identification Number (PIN). The application of ATM technology bypasses the need to build a complete bank branch and provides self-service banking with the ability to make transactions outside regular banking hours.

In the US, the first ATM launched was in Long Island, New York in 1969 by Chemical Bank. The link up of proprietary ATM networks was spurred by the US laws restricting financial institutions to local roles within a particular region. The development of ATM/cash cards began on a competitive, bank-by-bank basis. Over time, competitive pressure to provide ATM service on an extended geographical scope grew, leading to the integration of proprietary network ATMs. The driving forces behind the interconnected ATM networks were the two major credit card companies, Visa and MasterCard. Beginning in the early 1980s, Visa established the Plus network, while MasterCard created the

Cirrus standard. In 1991, Visa and MasterCard linked up their respective ATM networks.

Table 1.1 shows that the characteristics of the innovation process of ATM/cash cards in the UK were similar to those in the US, where developments progressed from stand-alone proprietary networks towards reciprocally-linked proprietary ATM networks. This chapter will now focus on the UK ATM/cash card innovation.

Table 1.1 Characteristics of the innovation process of ATM/cash cards in the US and the UK

	USA	UK
Competition (proprietary network)	Single bank system: Mellon Bank Data Centre, Philadephia National Bank, Bank of America, City National Bank	Barclays, Lloyds, NatWest, Midland, Halifax
Collaboration (integration of proprietary networks)	Regional ATM network: PULSE, HONOR, MOST STAR, National ATM network: Plus, Cirrus	Four Banks, Mint, LINK, Matrix
Innovation process characteristics	• Local, regional networks • Collaborative approach adopted in the mid-1970s • Less authoritative – PIN digits depending on the issuers	• National networks • Collaborative approach adopted in mid-1980s • More authoritative – rigid rules on number of digits in a PIN
Reasons for the joining of proprietary ATM networks	• The link up of proprietary ATM networks was according to the law for operation on a regional basis	• The link up of proprietary ATM networks was enabled by the Building Societies Act 1986
	• Defensive strategy to protect an institution's existing market share	• Offensive strategy of building societies to challenge the major banks in money transmission
	• Capital/technical resource constraints	• Capital/technical resource constraints

Source: Summarised from Essinger (1987).

ATM/cash card innovations in the UK

The history of ATM/cash card innovation in the UK began in 1967, when Barclays linked the note-dispensing machines provided by De La Rue to interface with the bank's accounting system to offer cash dispensing services to customers. The process of adopting the ATM technology was undertaken by Barclays' Management Services Department. The proprietary ATM network of Barclays was known as BarclayCash.[1] BarclayCash was a voucher system which used paper vouchers to feed into a machine in return for a single £10 note. At that time, other banks used machines which accepted thin plastic cards. These early machines simply used pre-encoded holes on the voucher or card to compare with the Personal Identification Number (PIN). However, there were major problems with these early cards. The cards were both insecure and unreliable; the machines were not connected to the bank's computers, so the ATM machines could not check whether the voucher (or card) had been reported as being lost or stolen and whether the customer had enough money in the account before dispensing the cash.

Table 1.2 shows the cost of establishing and maintaining ATM machines. In order to break even against the cost of ATM provision, each ATM needs around 3,750 transactions per month.[2] The cost of cash withdrawal through ATMs is 65 percent

Proprietary ATM network is the ATM channel established by any single financial institution to serve its customers. A proprietary ATM network can help promote the brand. Examples of proprietary ATM networks in the UK are BarclayCash service offered by Barclays, Cashpoint service offered by Lloyds, Servicetill service offered by NatWest, Autobank service offered by Midland, Cardcash service offered by Halifax, Abbeylink service offered by Abbey National and Cashlink service offered by Nationwide. However, a proprietary ATM network requires heavy investment in order to provide an extensive service coverage. Facing the problem of providing convenient coverage to cardholders, financial institutions later entered into collaboration to form a shared network, such as LINK, Matrix, Four Banks and Mint.

Innovation process

1960

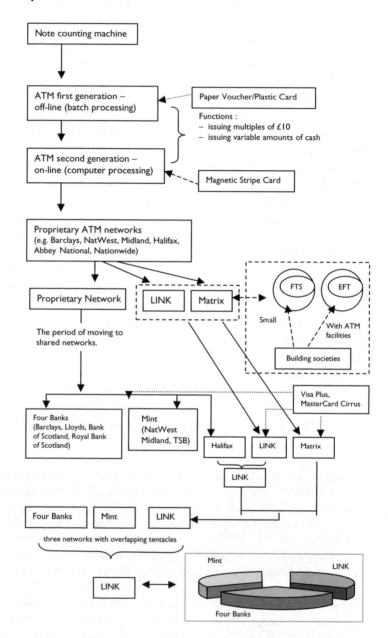

2002

Figure 1.1 The development of the ATM/cash card innovation
Source: The author's design.

Table 1.2   Cost per LINK ATM in 1998

	Cost of ATM per year (pounds)	Cost per ATM withdrawal (pence)
Fully burdened	25,116	29.3
Marginal	12,326	16.4

Source: LINK cited in Cruickshank (2000, p. 284).

of the cost of withdrawal at the counter. Furthermore, the cost per transaction for ATM withdrawals was 25–50 pence, cheaper than the cost of 65 pence for cheque-clearing between two different banks (Smith and Wield, 1988, p. 265).

A means to deliver an effective bank card system began with the launch of BarclayCash in 1967. The ATM service was first offered at Barclays' Enfield branch. At its launch, Barclays intended to use ATMs for cost reduction in place of using branch delivery for encashment services. The ATMs were not competing for deposit share.[3] Lloyds and the other innovators followed with the launch of the proprietary networks from the 1970s onwards (table 1.3).

Lloyds' Cashpoint ATMs were the on-line machines developed by IBM and regarded as second generation machines. These ATMs used plastic cards with a magnetic stripe which identified the customer's account. These machines were connected directly to the bank's central computers, and each withdrawal was checked against a hotlist and against the customer's balance

Table 1.3   The launch of ATM services by major financial institutions

Financial Institution	ATM service	Supplier	Year of Operation	ATM function
Barclays	BarclayCash	De La Rue	1967	Off-line
	BarclayBank	NCR	1975	On-line
Lloyds	Cashpoint	IBM	1972	On-line
NatWest	Servicetill	NCR	1975	On-line, off-line
Midland	Autobank	NCR	1979	On-line, off-line
Halifax	Cardcash	Philips	1983	On-line, real time
Abbey National	Abbeylink	NCR	1985	On-line, real time
Nationwide	Cashlink	NCR	1985	On-line, real time

before dispensing the cash. This meant that the new ATM machine was more secure than the old off-line machine. As the issuers in this period began to invest in ATMs to run their first proprietary networks, there were some major technological difficulties. The main problems concerned the integrity of the PIN within the computer system and the ability to ensure the correct identification of the authorised initiator of the transaction releasing transactions from an account. The networks of ATMs were insecure and unreliable; the network downtime averaged between 2 percent and 3 percent. The early machines also had a problem concerning their note handling capabilities, in that the machines required new or best-quality notes (Chorafas, 1988, pp. 205–19). The early mechanical problems also saw less money than requested being dispensed, phantom withdrawals and repeated machine breakdowns.[4]

The standard for the ATM cards using magnetic stripe technology was recommended by the International Organisation of Standards (ISO) so that cards from different payment systems could be accepted at the same terminal. There are three standard

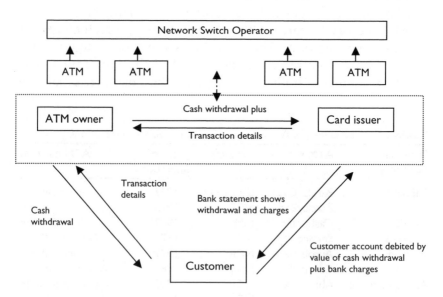

Figure 1.2   Parties involved in the link up of proprietary ATM networks
Source: Based on Cruickshank (2000, p. 279) in *Banking Review*.

tracks on an ATM card. Cards for use in on-line systems use track two to identify the cards to the computer whereas those for use in off-line working additionally use track three to carry the customer's PIN and the updateable withdrawal record. The encryption formula of the PIN is usually based on the US Data Encryption Standard (DES) encryption algorithm developed by IBM. The ATM technology is commercially driven by suppliers such as IBM, Diebold and NCR. ATM software is supplied by niche suppliers; most ATM networks use a system known as Base 24 developed by Shared Financial Systems.

Figure 1.2 represents the main parties involved in the link up of proprietary ATM networks. These are the *ATM owner* (acquirer) who dispenses the cash, the *card issuer* who operates the account from which money is withdrawn and the *network switch operator* who provides the switching service between different institutions' proprietary ATMs (Cruickshank, 2000, p. 279).

Table 1.4 shows the capacity of major banks in relation to ATM supply in 1982. Lloyds (later Lloyds TSB) led adoption, owning nearly 50 percent of the total number of ATMs. In the early 1980s, banks began to compete for market share in the retail deposit market by increasing investment in ATMs. The growth in terms of ATMs by up to 50 percent per year during the 1980s is shown in figure 1.3.

The link up of proprietary ATM networks began from 1986 onwards (tables 1.5 and 1.6). This was encouraged by the Building Society Act 1986, which permitted the owning and sharing of ATMs among building societies.[5] Taking into account the impact of the Building Societies Act, the number of ATMs installed by the building societies increased by 218 percent (from 652 in 1985 to 2,072 in 1987) and the current account balance also

Base 24 is the computer software used by a variety of financial institutions for processing on-line ATM transactions. A Base 24 system generally runs on a front end system, controls the physical ATM terminals, interfaces to the host system and provides 24-hour operation. The financial institutions use a Base 24 system for ATM inter-connection as they expand the ATM network. Base 24 software also enables the multi-bank-inter-linked ATM network.

Table 1.4 The capacity of major banks to meet demand for ATM supply in 1982

Financial Institutions	No. of ATMs	Current Account Balance (£millions)	Total Deposits Balance (£millions)	No. of ATM Cards
Lloyds TSB	1,119	4,898	27,856	2,271
NatWest	341	7,478	44,193	1,800
Barclays	207	—¹	38,302	1,765
Midland	193	5,046	28,623	883
Other	416	n/a	12,575	1,457
Total	2,276	29,990	151,549	8,176

Source: British Bankers' Association; The Retail Management Development Programme (1983); The Bankers (1982); Company annual reports.

¹ The figures in the Company Annual Report do not break down into current account balance.

increased by 24 percent (from £103,899 million to £129,331 million during the same period).[6]

Having seen the trend towards integration of ATM networks among smaller competitors as a threat to their size advantage, the large banks switched to a collaborative approach by forming the Four Banks network in 1987 and the Mint network in 1989. Disadvantaged by the emergence of the integrated proprietary

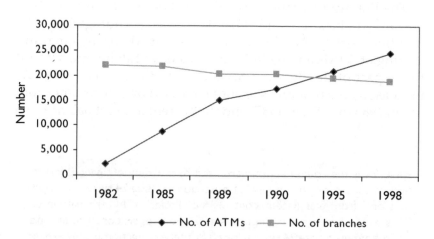

Figure 1.3 Bank branches and installed ATMs in the UK
Source: APACS (1999); *Banking World*; British Bankers' Association.

Table 1.5 The link up of proprietary ATM networks

ATM networks	Members	Year of operation
LINK	33 financial institutions, including the founding members of Abbey National, Nationwide Building Society, Co-operative Bank, Girobank, Funds Transfer Sharing (FTS)	1986
Matrix	Network of building societies – Alliance & Leicester, Anglia, Bradford & Bingley, Bristol & West, Leeds Permanent, National & Provincial, Woolwich, Electronic Fund Transfer (EFT) Ltd.	1986
Four Banks	Barclays, Lloyds, Royal Bank of Scotland and Bank of Scotland	1987
Mint	Midland, National Westminster, TSB, Clydesdale and Northern banks	1989

Source: APACS (1999); *Banking World*, July, p. 28; LINK Interchange Network; *Banking World*, 1987, p. 17.

Table 1.6 The number of ATMs according to ATM networks in the UK

	MINT	Four Banks	LINK	Proprietary
1988	—	3,873	971	3,695
1989	5,247	4,747	2,485	1,266
1990	6,000	5,350	4,504	827
1991	6,291	5,826	5,001	818
1992	6,330	6,107	5,603	833
1993	6,373	6,286	5,895	815
1994	6,440	6,536	6,228	829
1995	8,290	7,562	8,809	788
1996	9,843	9,113	11,729	735
1997	10,744	9,408	14,819	22
1998	11,118	9,852	19,393	20
1999	11,576	10,222	27,272	10
2000	0	0	31,979	9

Source: LINK Interchange Network.

ATM networks, Halifax, who had by far the largest number of ATMs among the building societies (917 ATMs), also joined LINK in 1988. In 1989, LINK merged with Matrix.

Table 1.7 Shared ATM networks in the UK

LINK Network

Abbey National plc.	Chelsea Building Society	National Australia Group
Airdrie Savings Bank	Citibank/Diners International	National Westminster Bank plc
Alliance & Leicester Group	Co-operative Bank plc	Nationwide Building Society
Allied Irish Banks plc	Coventry Building Society	Northern Rock plc
American Express Europe Ltd	Cumberland Building Society	Norwich & Peterborough Building Society
Bank of Scotland	Derbyshire Building Society	The Royal Bank of Scotland plc
Birmingham Midshires Building Society	Dunfermline Building Society	Sainsbury's Bank plc
Barclays Bank plc	Halifax plc	TSB Bank plc
Bradford & Bingley Building Society	HFC Bank plc	Woolwich plc
Bristol & West plc	Lloyds Bank plc	Yorkshire Building Society
Britannia Building Society	Midland Bank plc	

Four Banks Network

Bank of Scotland	Barclays Bank plc	Lloyds Bank plc
The Royal Bank of Scotland plc		

MINT Network

Midland Bank plc	National Westminster Bank plc	TSB Bank plc

Other institutions have bilateral arrangements with these banks, including Clydesdale Bank plc.

Source: APACS (1999, p. 24); LINK Interchange Network Ltd.

Four Banks Network is the shared ATM network formed in 1987 by Lloyds, Barclays, Bank of Scotland and Royal Bank of Scotland. The money transmission of the card business was controlled by these big four banks. They dominated around 90 percent and 80 percent of the UK ATM delivery system in the 1970s and 1980s respectively (The Retail Management Development Programme, 1983; Bank for International Settlements, 1989).

Table 1.8 ATM functions in terms of usage (as percentage of total usage)

Transaction	Usage
Cash dispensing	60
Deposit/payment	30
Transfer and enquiry	10

Source: Chorafas (1988, p. 206).

Table 1.8 demonstrates the operating statistic of one financial institution regarding the use of the ATM function. Provision of wide ATM access to customers is a key factor in the battle for retail banking customers.[7] Table 1.9 shows the share of innovators in respect of number of ATMs and current account balances. It can be seen that Lloyds TSB, the leading early adopter of ATMs, has the largest share of current account balances.

In the 1990s, banks attempted to expand the scope of ATM-based services by linking up with the other networks. For example, the Royal Bank of Scotland's joint venture (2.5% stake) with Banco Santander in Spain in 1989[8] and Midland's reciprocity with the Eurocheque Card network in 1990.[9] LINK also developed a gateway to Europay/Mastercard in 1993.[10]

With regards to the link up of proprietary ATM networks, there are two types of transaction charges: switch fees and interchange fees. Switch fees are paid to the operator of the central

Mint Network is the shared ATM network formed in 1989. The Mint project links the ATM networks of Midland (now HSBC), NatWest and the TSB. Subsequent to a series of bank mergers in the 1990s, Mint then joined the LINK network by the end of 1998.

Table 1.9 Share of ATMs and current account balances by major banks

No. of ATMs

	1985	1989	1990	1995	1998	Average share from 1985–1998 (%)
Lloyds TSB	2,864	4,095	4,464	4,346	4,277	22
NatWest	2,022	2,583	2,645	2,998	3,285	15
Barclays	887	2,193	2,276	3,020	3,218	14
Midland/HSBC	1,081	1,868	1,908	2,282	2,792	11
Other	1,991	4,305	6,051	8,254	11,002	
Total	8,845	15,044	17,344	20,900	24,574	

Current account balance (£millions)

	1985	1989	1990	1995	1998	Average share from 1985–1998 (%)
Lloyds TSB	—[1]	12,494	16,940	52,504	63,381	17
NatWest	10,213	19,482	22,271	37,727	45,388	14
Barclays	8,604	10,457	14,604	34,943	41,884	12
Midland/HSBC	11,175	13,851	19,456	34,551	35,818	12
Other	—	51,579	42,549	96,602	204,829	
Total	51,722	107,863	115,820	256,327	391,300	

Source: Credit Lyonnais Securities Europe (UK); British Bankers' Association; APACS (1999, p. 42); Company annual reports.

[1] The figures in the Company annual report do not break down into current account balance.

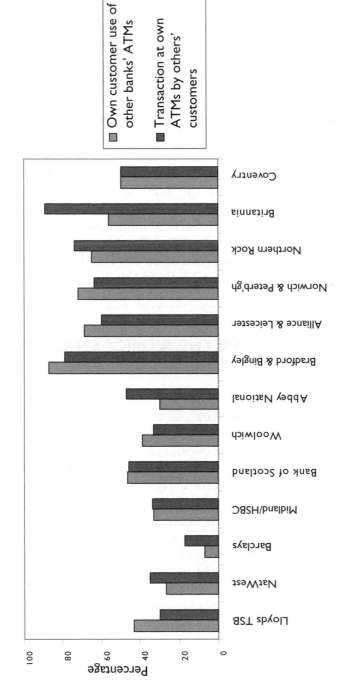

Figure 1.4 The proportion of transactions at ATMs by other banks' customers
Source: Cruickshank (2000).

switching infrastructure and range from 1 to 3 pence per transaction. Interchange fee charges are paid by card issuers to ATM owners when their customers use ATMs owned by an ATM acquirer. The interchange fee is 28 pence for branch-based machines and 40 pence for off-site machines (Cruickshank, 2000, pp. 284, 286). The proportion of ATM transactions by customers using the other banks' ATMs against customers using their own bank's ATMs are shown in figure 1.4. It can be seen that these proportionate transactions are more or less the same for all innovators.

Table 1.10 shows the growth of ATMs in the UK, which supports the argument that the bank card innovation has achieved a level of diffusion.

Figure 1.5 shows the market shares of innovators in the current account market in 1998. Lloyds TSB still held the highest share with 23 percent. Figure 1.6 shows that the Big Four clearing banks (Barclays, Lloyds TSB, NatWest, Midland/HSBC) take the largest share in terms of number of ATM machines and cards.

COMPETITION IN THE ATM/CASH CARD MARKET

Figure 1.7 shows how the progress of innovation was shaped by the strategy of banks and building societies. The outer circle represents the revenue pool for the innovation. The inner circle represents the size of the market share of individual banks or building societies. In the early innovation period, banks and building societies competed to launch proprietary ATM networks. However, the scope of ATM/cash card usage was limited since the cards could only be used within the banks or building societies' own ATM network. Therefore, ATM/cash cards were failing to meet the needs of increasingly mobile customers. By entering into collaboration to form integrated proprietary ATM networks, banks and building societies could enjoy the external benefits (the extended scope of ATM-based service).

Competition in ATM service began in the 1980s. Figure 1.3, and tables 1.4 and 1.9, demonstrate the aggressive investment made

Table 1.10 The growth of ATMs in the UK

	1975	1980	1985	1990	1991	1992	1993	1998
No. of ATMs	568	1,707	8,845	17,344	18,136	18,652	19,140	24,574
Increase (%)	—	201	418	96	5	3	3	28
No. of ATM cards	583	4,732	19,801	25,200	27,200	26,948	26,580	23,747
Increase (%)	—	712	318	27	8	–1	–1	–11
No. of transactions through ATMs (millions)	8	55	404	1,012	1,085	1,169	1,242	1,850
Increase (%)	—	588	635	150	7	8	6	49
Value of transactions through ATMs (£million)	111	1,316	12,401	43,262	47,937	55,975	60,200	98,230
Increase (%)	—	1,086	842	249	11	17	8	63

Source: APACS Yearbook of Payment Statistics (1995, 1996, 1999).

Share of current account customers
(in millions)

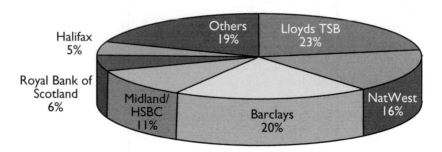

Figure 1.5 Share of current account customers by major financial institutions in 1998

Source: Datamonitor.

Share of ATM/cash card market 1998
(by number of ATM machines)

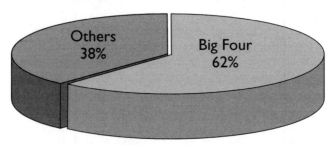

Share of ATM/cash card market
(by number of ATM cards)

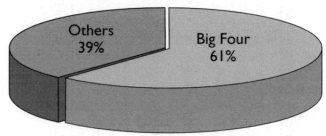

Figure 1.6 Share of the Big Four banks – number of ATM machines and cards
Source: APACS (1999); Key Note Market Report (1999) – Credit & Other Finance Cards.

in ATMs by major banks during 1982–9. Lloyds TSB increased investment in ATMs by 266%; NatWest by 657%; Barclays by 959%; and Midland/HSBC by 868%. Their investment reflects the drive to provide an efficient and quality cash withdrawal service. The banks saw that competitive advantage in the ATM market was difficult to obtain because ATM service was tied to current account customers. Therefore, the banks tended to focus on employing ATM technology to better serve and retain their customers.

Since the introduction of the Building Societies Act 1986 removed the restrictions previously placed upon building societies, enabling them to own and share ATMs, the banks' pursuit of competitive strategy (through a proprietary ATM network) transformed into collaborative strategy (the integration of proprietary ATM networks). With the integration of LINK and Matrix in 1986, the individual banks faced the possibility of competing open networks becoming a competitive threat to their position. Even though individual banks did not originally intend to collaborate (table 1.3), they soon realised that collaboration was a necessary approach to avoid being left at a competitive disadvantage. Thus, they linked up their ATMs with the competing networks to form the Four Banks and Mint networks (tables 1.5,

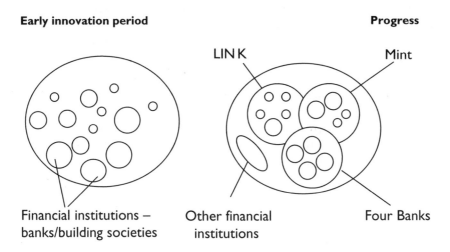

Early innovation period　　　　　　　　　　　　　　**Progress**

LINK　　　　　　　　　Mint

Financial institutions –　　Other financial　　　　Four Banks
banks/building societies　　institutions

Figure 1.7　The progress of innovation in the context of innovators' strategy – ATM/cash cards

1.6 and 1.7). The pursuit of a collaborative strategy helped the individual banks to achieve the external benefits offered by the extended scope of ATM-based service (figure 1.7).

Although Barclays was the first to deliver an ATM-based service, it secured no particular competitive advantage. This was because its Barclaycash system was operated off-line and suffered from many technical problems.[11] Other banks, as later entrants could then employ on-line ATM technology to overtake Barclays. Since the Halifax Cardcash network was by far the largest non-bank network, Halifax was confident that it could exploit its large network to gain a competitive advantage over building society competitors. However, under competitive pressures from the link up of proprietary ATM networks, Halifax failed to achieve any significant commercial advantage. Lloyds TSB, too, failed to gain a competitive edge, despite owning the largest installed base of ATMs (tables 1.4 and 1.9). This is because other competitors invested in ATMs to narrow the gap in terms of the number of ATMs (table 1.9). Even though Lloyds TSB's ATM network was superior to most of its competitors, the share of current account balances (table 1.9) and current account customers (figure 1.5) shows that Lloyds TSB had no real benefits from its relative advantage in proprietary ATMs.

Taking into account the benefits in terms of interchange fees (figure 1.4), the proportion of transactions at ATMs by rival banks' customers is more or less the same as the proportion of transactions of same-bank customers using other innovators' (banks/building societies) ATMs. The proportionate transactions suggest that no single innovator gained competitive advantage from net interchange fees.[12] Moreover, the ability to use their current account base to cross-sell other banking products is common among innovators. Thus, there is no indication that any innovator could achieve competitive advantage in the case of the ATM/cash card innovation.

SUMMARY

The ATM/cash cards case study has shown that the technology behind the innovation is not complex. The ATM technology, software and networking technologies can be purchased from a third- party operator (technology push product). In other words, the launch of proprietary ATM services is not difficult since innovators could similarly buy the required technology if they chose to do so. The provision of a cash withdrawal service only involved connecting current accounts via the banks' networking and data communication for interbranch service. However, the problem lies in the strategy towards owning customers. There are difficulties in respect of service differentiation since the provision of a money withdrawal service was the same across the financial service providers as a result of a common technology across innovators. Therefore, in order to satisfy customers' demands for widely available cash provisioning from the ATM-based service, innovators needed to employ the strategies of cooperative competition.

The banks and building societies did not see collaboration as necessary until the enactment of the Building Societies Act 1986. Intensified competition in the 1980s was due to the introduction of the Building Societies Act 1986, which allowed the building societies to own and share ATMs. Banks' strategy of using ATMs for cost reduction began to change into competing for a share in the retail deposit market. The banks and building societies saw collaboration as an opportunity to extend the service coverage. Also, small financial institutions could be more competitive by piggy backing on the infrastructure provided by the larger banks to compete for the share of deposits. To get a substantial ATM network up and running for an effective level of ATM service coverage, collaboration is needed in terms of linking up with the competing networks. A collaborative approach was, therefore, considered by the banks and building societies as the cheapest route to providing customers with a comprehensive ATM network. Collaboration was involved in terms of the cooperative price setting over switch and interchange fees for using each other's ATM networks. Thus, the development of the ATM innovation led to the process of integrating proprietary ATM networks.

Given the combined effect of the increased competition in the 1980s and the changes in legislation, the dominant status of major banks in the ATM market seemed to be under threat. Competitive pressure was exerted through the creation of shared networks to match those created by competitors. Innovators entered into collaboration in international networks to expand the geographical scope of service.

The integration to form the shared network, whereby any innovator could join, then became an open system. This open system allows the innovator to enjoy the benefits in terms of expanded ATM scope of service, that is, the card issued by one financial institution can be used for cash withdrawal at other network members. However, the open system still failed to present innovators with sufficient commercial maneuverability to attain a competitive advantage.

Credit Cards

The credit card is a variable repayment card which offers a line of credit to the cardholder who can spend up to a pre-arranged ceiling level. The extended credit must be settled within a given period, or else interest will be charged on the remaining balance (Paxson and Wood, 1998, p. 52). The innovation of the credit card in this book is in the context of the development of an electronic card payment network which provides the credit extension to the cardholders at the point of sale by using a swipe card. Credit cards effectively provide a self-service loan through a non-bank service outlet, for example, through retailers, and will play a key role in support of e-business.

Credit card innovations

The first form of a credit card system originated in the US in the form of credit documents constructed from card. Later, at the beginning of the twentieth century, embossed metal addressograph plates were used by Western Union and other banks to identify customers and record details of their accounts. In 1947, the Flatbush National Bank introduced its 'Charge-it' plan, a monthly charge account restricted to customers of the bank, and in 1951 the Franklin National Bank became the first bank to issue credit cards to customers of rival banks (Lindsey, 1994, p. 129; A Report on the Supply of Credit Card Franchise Services in the United Kingdom, 1980, p. 7). However, the first modern credit card appeared in 1950, when Diners Club launched the Travel and Entertainment (T&E) card. This was followed by American Express in 1958, which featured a credit period between expenditure and settlement but had no facility for roll-over credit or part payment.

The credit card innovation, stimulated by regulatory restrictions on inter-state bank branching, provided the first national banking product in the US. Even so, collaborative development of cards was needed, to provide recognition of cards outside local regions, as the card issuing bank's range, inter-state, was limited in terms of communication and funding. A national credit card was created in 1966 when the Bank of America licensed its credit cards to other banks across the US and overseas. Disturbed by the leadership position BankAmericard had created, rival banks joined together in the same year to create a competitive system under the name of Interbank, which later became MasterCharge and then MasterCard (Frazer, 1985, pp. 16–17; Vartanian et al., 1998, p. 56).

The development of the credit card in subsequent decades has been dominated by the systems supported by Visa and

BankAmericard was a credit card launched by the Bank of America. It was the first revolving credit card marketed all across the US. The Bank of America set up BankAmericard Service Corporation which undertook the licensing of its schemes for a fee to other banks: the Corporation maintained a tight control over the issuing of its cards. The scheme was successful because bankers avoided the complexities of starting their own programmes and cardholders found they could use their BankAmericard when they travelled to other states. In 1966, Barclays imported the entire operation of the BankAmericard system, including the computer program and the terms and conditions of service for UK credit card processing.

Innovation Process

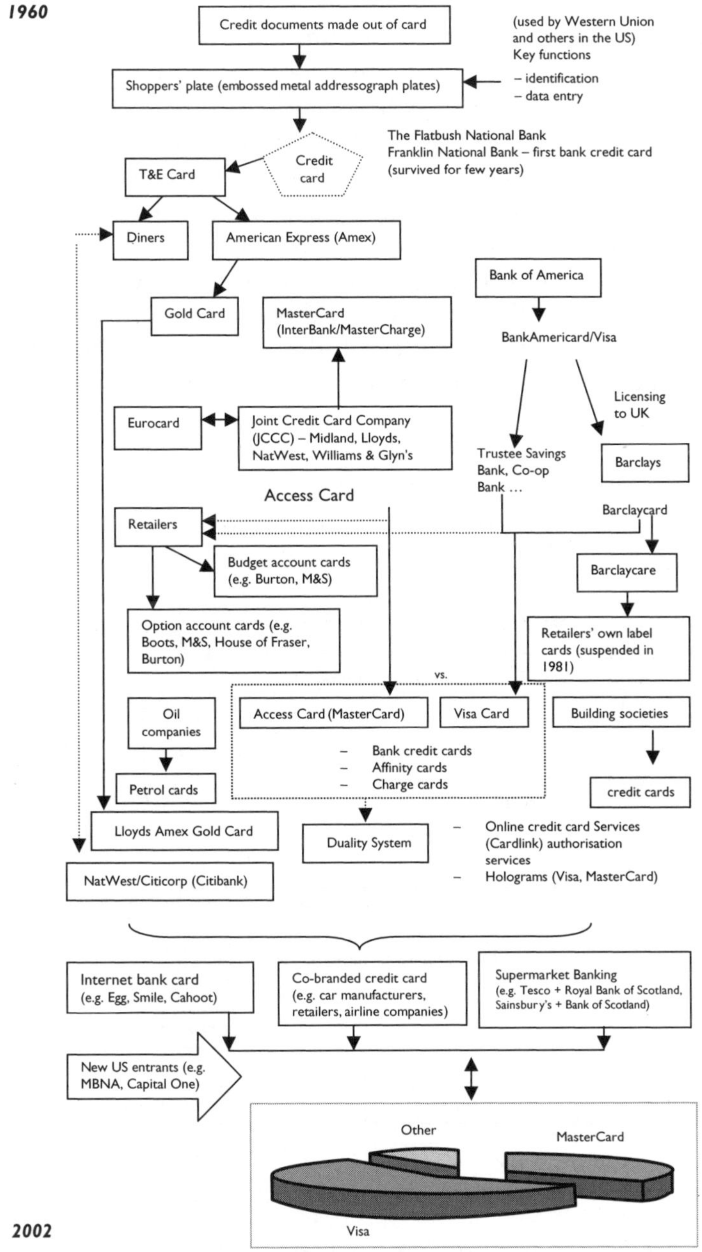

1960

Figure 2.1 The development of the credit card innovation
Source: The author's design.

MasterCard. Visa and MasterCard have standards covering the card design, location and contents of the magnetic stripe tracks, the rules for authorisation, clearing and settlement of transactions. One of the most difficult problems in the early stages of card development was how to develop an effective and cost-efficient authorisation system. The early success of the credit cards created heavy delays on dedicated telecommunication lines and thus required the development of sophisticated 'switching' technology (Mandell, 1990, p. 61). Two computer networks were established for interchange (the clearing of credit card transactions) to provide 24-hour-a-day credit authorisation – MasterCard's version called INET (Interbank Network for Electronic Transfer), and Visa's equivalent, BASE-I (Lindsey, 1994, p. 132).

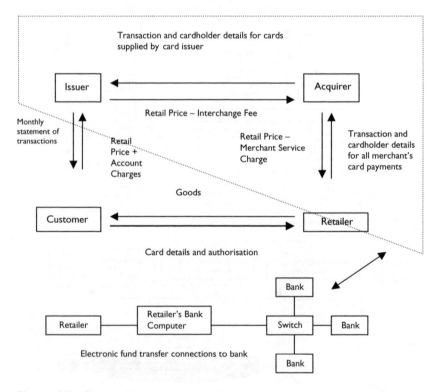

Figure 2.2   Parties involved in the credit card system
Source: Based on *Banking Review* in Cruickshank (2000, p. 252) and SAE in Retail Management Development Programme (1983).

Table 2.1 Comparative costs to society of cash, cheques and credit cards, US and UK (US cents per transaction)

Country	Source	Year	Cash	Cheques	Credit cards	Ratio cards/ cheques
US	Arthur D. Little	Mid-1970s	1.4	29	55	1:21
	Hamilton-Budd	1976	1.2	53	52	1:44
UK	IBRO	1974	1.2–2.4	40	—	1:34–1:17

Source: Cited by Williamson (1981, p. 230); there is a printer's error in the source for the cost of cash in the UK in OECD (1983).
Note: The comparison is not valid because the grant of credit without charging credit costs to customers (cardholders) is the characteristic of the debit card innovation. The basis of the comparisons (free credit) is unclear.

In 1966, Barclays made an arrangement with the Bank of America to issue credit cards in the UK. Barclays imported the entire operation, including the computer programs and the terms and conditions of service to both retailers and cardholders. A computer program change was all that was needed to modify the Bank of America program for UK purposes.

Figure 2.2 shows the main parties involved in a credit card system. These are the *card issuer*, who supplies the cards to the customer and operates the account from which payment is made, the *retailer* (merchant), who exchanges goods or services for the customer's card details and consent to make the payment, and the *merchant acquirer*, who recruits retailers to the scheme, reimburses the retailer and obtains funds from the card issuer. The issuer has two sources of revenue from card transactions: revenue from the customer, such as annual fees and interest payments; and interchange fees[1] paid by merchant acquirers. The merchant acquirer derives revenue from service charges to the merchant.[2]

IBM introduced a magnetic stripe in plastic bank cards in 1969. The banking organisations agreed to the International Standards Organisation (ISO) 7811, Parts 4 and 5, covering encoding requirements, layout and recording density. The first track followed standards set by the International Air Transport Association (IATA), while the second track followed the format set by the American Bankers' Association (ABA) (Mandell, 1990, pp. 143–4).

A comparative study of the cost of credit cards compared with the paper-based system was conducted by Arthur D. Little and Hamilton-Budd in the US and UK. The results presented in table 2.1 suggest credit cards do not provide cheaper processing costs than cheques, although comparisons are distorted by the credit-free period promoted on most cards.

The first step towards developing a functional credit card network in the UK began in 1966 when Barclays issued a blue, white and gold card – Barclaycard (A Report on the Supply of Credit Card Franchise Services in the United Kingdom, 1980, p. 17). At the time of the launch of Barclaycard, the entire UK processing system was still paper-based. However, as the credit card market grew (table 2.2), Barclaycard commissioned a new computer system in 1974 called UKII to overcome the inefficiency of a paper-based system, provide a faster authorisation service for member merchants and branches, and supply monthly statements for cardholders.[3] This system was finally updated to the UKIII system in April 1983.[4]

To provide a quality credit card service, Barclays built up its retailer base for credit card acceptance. In the early years of its launch, Barclaycard increased the number of cardholders at a rate of 20 percent per year and its initial success enabled it to gain the largest share of the UK market (table 2.2). Barclaycard's success stimulated competitors into launching their own cards. In 1972, a dual credit card operation called the Joint Credit Card Company Limited (JCCC) was formed by National Westminster, Lloyds, Midland and Williams & Glyn's banks to compete with Barclaycard. Also known by its brand name, Access, the infrastructure of the JCCC was funded 30 percent each by Lloyds, Midland and NatWest and 10 percent by the Royal Bank of Scotland/Williams & Glyn's Group (Lindsey, 1994, p. 138). To launch the Access card, a computer program was purchased from the US and then rewritten for Access purposes. The trader base was set up, with IBM equipment installed at each sale location in

UKII was a computer system for credit card processing. The use of UKII eliminated much of the paperwork and provided a monthly statement for cardholders.

Table 2.2 The major credit card companies – number of outlets and cards

Year	Barclaycard		Access cards		American Express	
	Outlets ('000)	Cards (millions)	Outlets ('000)	Cards (millions)	Outlets ('000)	Cards (millions)
1970	45	1.3	—	—	8	0.04
1971	49	1.7	—	—	10	0.05
1972	61	2.0	—	—	12	0.08
1973	76	2.4	—	—	13	0.11
1974	82	2.9	—	—	14	0.16
1975	87	3.3	97	3.2	17	0.20
1976	92	3.5	100	2.6	21	0.26
1977	100	3.8	107	3.12	26	0.33
1978	115	4.5	123	3.63	31	0.41
1979	131	4.9	142	4.09	36	0.51

Source: A Report on the Supply of Credit Card Franchise Services in the United Kingdom (1980, pp. 37–8, 70–1, 95); Barclaycard Media Information.

1972. In 1973, the JCCC expanded its network by purchasing a 15 percent stake in Eurocard.[5] The JCCC then joined what is now MasterCard in 1974, so that they could offer their customers the vast global coverage advantage of the MasterCard network, allowing for full reciprocity for cardholders and merchants worldwide (Frazer, 1985, p. 266; Lindsey, 1994, p. 31).

Table 2.2 shows the number of outlets and cards for the major credit card companies. From the data given, it is clear that Barclaycard held the strongest position in terms of number of retail outlets and cards issued in the early 1970s.

Table 2.3 Market share of the credit card companies in the UK in terms of gross transaction turnover (in percentages)

	1974	1975	1976	1977	1978	1979
Access	27.8	34.3	34.6	34.4	35.8	35.7
Barclaycard	48.2	46	43.9	40.7	39.8	39
American Express	14.5	12.2	14.7	18	17.8	17.1
Diners Club	8.6	6.7	6.2	6.3	5.8	5.2
Others	0.9	0.8	0.6	0.6	0.8	3
Total	100	100	100	100	100	100

Source: A Report on the Supply of Credit Card Franchise Services in the United Kingdom (1980, p. 187).

The 1970s saw strong competition between Barclaycard and Access to acquire new cardholders with the credit card companies achieving 50,000 and 62,000 new customers per month respectively.[6] In 1977, Barclays joined the Visa network to expand the scope of its card usage.[7] In the 1980s, competition intensified as the popularity of cards encouraged retailers to launch their own credit card schemes (Worthington, 1992), and in 1988, the duality system allowing banks to join both Visa and MasterCard credit card networks became possible.

In the UK, the Big Four clearing banks are major issuers (80% of the market) as well as acquirers (90% of the market).[8] Throughout the 1980s and 1990s, Barclays continued to hold the largest market share in the credit card market.

Table 2.4 shows the growth of credit card market from the 1970s to the 1990s. Prior to 1988, banks had competed because they exclusively issued Visa or MasterCard credit cards. However, with the introduction of the duality system, there were clear benefits in terms of enhancing scale economies. Banks could now process all the Visa and MasterCard transactions of their merchants. Table 2.6 shows that Visa and MasterCard are the major players in the credit card industry, providing scale-based advantages in terms of the card processing operation, and supply an extensive network of distribution.

Table 2.4 The growth of credit cards in the UK

	1975	1980	1990	1991	1992	1993	1998
No. of credit cards ('000)	6,410	11,673	29,846	29,025	28,631	27,588	41,568
Increase (%)		82	156	−3	−1	−4	51
No. of transactions (millions)	59	150	693	690	715	738	1,224
Increase (%)		155	361	0	4	3	66
Value of transactions (£millions)	638	2,883	27,742	29,350	31,272	33,508	75,305
Increase (%)		352	862	6	7	7	125

Source: APACS Yearbook of Payment Statistics (1995, 1999); CLCB Statistical Unit, Abstract of Banking Statistics (in Frazer, 1985, p. 22).

Table 2.5 Credit card share of major financial institutions (in thousands of cards on issue)

	1985	1988	1990	1992	1994	1995	1996	1997	1998[1]
Barclays	7,947	9,007	9,900	8,090	8,464	8,944	9,273	9,429	9,561
Lloyds TSB	n/a	5,817	5,986	4,622	4,775	5,256	5,619	5,801	5,923
NatWest	2,669	4,606	5,226	3,450	3,556	3,654	3,834	4,502	4,655
Midland/HSBC	355	926	4,397	1,828	3,296	3,620	4,089	4,534	4,489
Other	615	1,457	1,910	2,079	2,601	3,742	4,640	7,563	8,165
Total	11,586	21,813	27,419	20,069	22,692	25,216	27,455	31,829	32,793

Source: British Bankers' Association; Key Note – Credit & Other Finance Cards (1999, p. 38).

[1] Estimated figures from Key Note.

Table 2.6 Number of credit and charge cards in issue in the UK ('000)

	1985	1987	1990	1992	1994	1995	1996	1997	1998
MasterCard	8,515	11,370	12,294	11,169	10,891	11,656	12,829	14,533	15,396
Visa	11,080	13,106	17,552	16,019	16,225	17,646	19,710	22,275	24,371
Others	—	—	—	1,442	1,340	1,476	1,599	1,635	1,801
Total	19,595	24,476	29,846	28,631	28,456	30,778	34,139	38,443	41,568

Source: APACS (1995, 1999).

Scale economies

The relative advantage of the scale of a corporation's network and its distribution channels results in increased accessibility to customers. Large scale operations may reduce unit costs, so that the output of a new larger plant is cheaper on average than the output from the smaller plant it replaced. For example, Barclays has scale advantage from being Europe's largest credit card issuer.

In the 1990s the level of competition in the credit card market increased as US card companies and new industry players such as auto makers and supermarket giants became significant issuers (table 2.7). The competitive environment and the share of credit card issuers in the UK credit card market in the 1990s are shown in figure 2.3.

Table 2.7   The types of new players in the UK credit card market in the 1990s

Type of players	Players in the UK market
Foreign entrants	American Express, Citibank, MBNA, HFC, Capital One, BankOne, Peoples Bank and The Associates
Non-financial institutions	Virgin, Vauxhall or General Motors (GM) card, AT&T Universal Card
Travel and entertainment	American Express, Diners Club
Specialist credit card issuers	MBNA, Capital One, and Household International
Retail and store cards	Tesco and Sainsbury, Marks & Spencer (branded loyalty card products)
Internet cards	Egg, Marbles, Smile, Cahoot

Source: The author's design.

Auto makers

In the competitive environment of the 1990s, non-financial institutions launched credit cards to compete with traditional banks. The auto maker cards, for example Virgin, Vauxhall or General Motors (GM) card, AT&T Universal Card, are the new players in the UK credit card market.

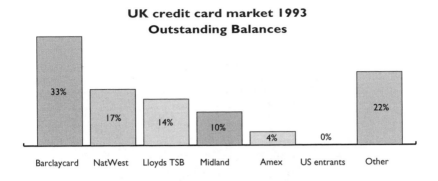

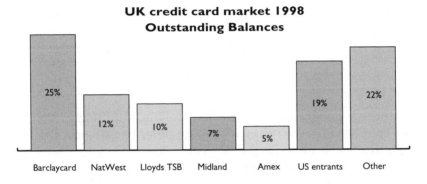

Figure 2.3 The shares in the UK credit card market
Source: Card Forum International, Jan./Feb. 2000, p. 51.

In the late 1990s, an Internet card (Egg card) was introduced by Prudential Banking in an attempt to take advantage of the growing volumes of Internet purchases. In the late 1990s, card issuers also entered into collaboration with specific partners in order to improve competitiveness by introducing customer-tailored variants to their products/services. For example, the collaborations between Lloyds TSB and Vodafone, Barclaycard and BT Cellnet, Woolwich and Vodafone, and NatWest and Orange in the form of a service agreement (a short-term contract of 2–3 years)[9] to offer mobile banking to customers, enabling the cardholders to access their bank accounts and make payments over mobile phones. Another example is the partnership between the Royal Bank of Scotland and Tesco, which featured a joint 50:50 venture to expand the Royal Bank of Scotland's card base beyond

**Share of credit card market 1998
(by number of credit cards)**

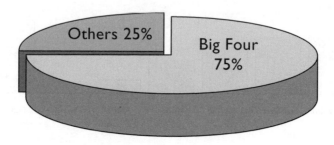

Figure 2.4 Share of credit card market of major banks compared with other industry players

Source: APACS (1999); Key Note Market Report (1999) – Credit & Other Finance Cards.

its limited geographical area in Scotland by using Tesco's customer base (as well as cross-selling other banking products).

Figure 2.4 shows that the Big Four clearing banks (Barclays, Lloyds TSB, NatWest, Midland/HSBC) are major issuers in the UK. Taking into account the credit cards issued, the percentage share of the credit card market taken by the Big Four was the largest (75 percent).

COMPETITION IN THE CREDIT CARD MARKET

Figure 2.5 shows how the development of the credit card was shaped by the innovators' strategy. Both outer circles represent the total revenue pool of innovation. The inner circles represent the market share of the individual card issuer. Barclaycard's early large market share was a result of its first-mover strategy. Barclaycard was not interested in joining the other networks since it had a strong credit card customer base which meant that it could offer internal benefits. Later, Barclaycard suffered from the effects of a shrinking market share stemming from competing

Early innovation period

Progress

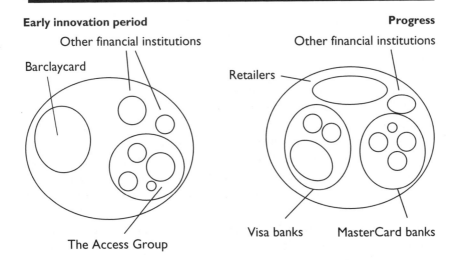

Figure 2.5 The development of innovation in the context of innovators' strategy – Credit cards

networks, and thus joined the Visa network, allowing Barclaycard to utilize some of the benefits from the expanded scope of credit card usage. In the case of the Access Group, joining together meant that the individual banks could overcome the constraints of their limited networks. Each individual bank could provide the extended scope of credit card service from the combined network of retail outlets. Obviously, as the banks, over time, entered the Visa or MasterCard network, they could also enjoy the extended scope of credit card service.

The competition between banks for market share began in the 1970s with Barclaycard achieving an initial competitive advantage. As Access planned to launch its set of cards in 1972, Barclaycard had by that point already acquired over 2 million cardholders and 61,000 merchant outlets (table 2.2). Preceding Access's launch by six years, Barclaycard had secured competitive advantage, enjoying a market share of around 40 percent throughout the 1970s (table 2.3). Although Barclaycard suffered 11 years of incurred losses and was not a profitable franchise until 1977, its name was synonymous with credit cards:[10] 81.5 percent of cardholders were Barclaycard customers (A Report on the Supply of Credit Card Franchise Services in the United Kingdom,

1980, pp. 38, 49). The large base of cardholders and brand strength enabled Barclaycard to launch a further range of financial services such as Barclaycard Platinum, Barclaycard Gold and Barclaycard MasterCard.[11] The name 'Barclaycard' was also a premium brand that enabled Barclaycard to charge higher APR rates than its mainstream competitors.[12]

Given Barclaycard's strong and competitive position, entry into a collaborative scheme was not foremost in the innovators' minds. However, the leading position of Barclaycard was eroded when the Access group entered the credit card business in 1972. The launch of Access threatened Barclaycard since the former group expanded their scope of service by joining the Eurocard and MasterCard networks. In response, Barclaycard linked up its credit card network with Visa, hoping to expand and defend its customer base.

Eventually the Visa and MasterCard networks evolved into an open system. The benefit to the participating players was in terms of expanding the scope of credit card usage (figure 2.5) without having to make any high level of investment. Under the open system, any card issuer can join the network, and therefore competitive advantage is given to no one. The competitive advantage instead has to come from the innovator's own strategy. Barclaycard's pursuit of first-mover strategy, for example, enabled it to enter the European credit card market in Germany, France and Spain. Barclaycard also pursued a collaborative strategy with BT Cellnet to launch the new mobile banking service. Hence, even though Barclaycard's share in the credit card market was undermined by the increasing competition in the 1980s from new entrants (like retailers), and in the 1990s from foreign card issuers, Barclaycard still maintained its leading role with the largest market share up to the late 1990s (figure 2.3).

Taking into account the market share in terms of number of cards issued in the credit card market (table 2.5), although the major players like Lloyds TSB, NatWest and Midland/HSBC gained substantial market shares, it was still around half the share held by Barclaycard.

SUMMARY

The case study of credit cards has shown the complexity in terms of network development. The credit card network had to involve the retailer business for credit fund transfer. The operation of a credit card system needs the credit authorisation initiated at the retailer's point of sale. The innovation requires network externalities to complete the core and peripheral functions of credit cards, including issuers, acquirers, merchants, hotels, insurance and car rental companies, etc. In other words, the card purchasing network will not be functional without the recruitment of merchants as credit card acceptance locations. The operation of a credit card network also needs a standard for the exchange and settlement of payment transactions (for passing messages for clearing, settlement and electronic fund transfer among issuing banks and merchant banks).

The complexity in the process of innovation comes from competition among alternative cards available in the marketplace; for example, the retail credit charge cards launched by merchants to compete with the traditional bank card issuers in the 1980s. The complexity in market competition also increased with respect to pricing (credit card interest rates). As a senior executive at one card issuer remarked, "The main barrier to entry of new credit card providers is the highly competitive and fragmented nature of the business, coupled with the present focus on rate driven offers. Clearly, rates offered at below the cost of funds are not sustainable. However, unless offers are competitive, it is difficult to achieve market share growth".

The change to the duality system in 1988, which allowed any bank to join both the Visa and MasterCard credit card networks, increased the competition further. The impact of issuing more types of credit cards as a result of membership of both Visa and MasterCard increased the number of persons holding more than one credit card. The main effect on competition was in terms of persuading the cardholders to use one credit card instead of another. Also, credit management became critical since the provision of revolving credit was not backed by the customers' deposit accounts.

Regarding innovators' strategies, the large size of the credit card market meant innovators faced difficulties in expanding an exclusive network of retail outlets by going alone. Therefore, innovators chose to link up with the Visa and MasterCard networks. The individual bank could provide the extended scope of credit card service from the combined network of retail outlets. Obviously, the banks could enjoy the benefits from the extended scope of credit card service. Eventually the Visa and MasterCard networks progressed into an open system. However, as any card issuer can join the network, the open system gives no competitive advantage. The competitive advantage of the innovator (card issuer) can be seen as coming from the innovator's own strategy. As can be seen from the case of Barclaycard, its pursuit of first-mover strategy created competitive advantage, which meant Barclaycard was able to maintain its leading role with the biggest market share up to the late 1990s. Barclaycard could establish its brand as almost a generic term for credit cards and was widely recognised by consumers. Barclaycard's strategy in the credit card market has been associated with three continuing elements. The first factor was the continued growth of the credit card market. The second factor was the relative success of Visa, whose UK franchise was exclusively enjoyed by Barclaycard in the early years. Barclaycard's Visa cards had international acceptability with 16 million merchants worldwide. The third factor was the ability to avoid price competition by branding and by use of new features supported by technology developments within the card networks. For example, the alliances with companies such as British Telecom and Cellnet allowed Barclaycard to develop improved products for mobile banking.

Barclaycard did not compete on price – its interest charges (APR) were not the lowest on offer. Barclaycard also marketed its products as a unique service. This differentiated Barclaycard from other high-street bank credit cards that were sold as another feature of the bank's service. It had invested heavily in an energetic and sustained promotion/advertising campaign; the investment in advertising was designed to send a message, emphasising peace of mind in case of an emergency (such as losing the card or passport), medical problems on holiday or losing goods purchased with Barclaycard. The leadership of

Barclaycard in the credit card market can be seen from its market share of 34 percent in terms of credit cards issued, and 27 percent in terms of transaction values, provided the company with a strong financial base.

EFTPOS/Debit Cards

HISTORY OF THE DEBIT CARD

The EFTPOS/debit card innovation is considered in this book as the development of a card-based electronic payment system which allows an instant payment directly debited from the customer's account by using debit cards (Paxson and Wood, 1998, p. 55). The introduction of EFTPOS/debit cards was intended to replace cash, cheque and credit transfers. Potentially, the EFTPOS/debit card also replaces credit cards on low budget transactions such as food retailing.

The innovation was based on collaboration as well as competition. In Denmark, a PIN-only, on-line-only network was supported by a unified debit card scheme and with retailer service provided through a central organisation. The scheme was successful since the banks offered free terminals and free transactions for an initial period. Hence the scheme became established with little resistance from retailers. However, in Belgium, where a similar unitary network was introduced by banks, retailers found that EFTPOS transaction volumes, and therefore charges, had risen with increased card use. Retailers collectively fought back by refusing to pay transaction charges

(Howells and Hine, 1993, p. 51). In France, the collaborative bank approach succeeded with the creation of the national electronic payment card system, the Groupement des Cartes Bancaires. There had previously been problems involving the EFTPOS experiments in France in the early 1980s as banks competed with each other to issue cards and acquire retailers, just as they had done under the EFTPOS system in the UK. A full system innovation was not inevitable in Germany; banks' attempts to introduce a centralised EFTPOS system since the early 1980s failed as a result of disagreement over the format for terminals. Its adoption was also hampered as the banks proposed a transaction charge of 0.3 percent of annual EFTPOS turnover (O'Hanlon and Rocha, 1993, p. 40).

The early 1980s also saw a gradual diffusion of EFTPOS across Europe. The development of EFTPOS systems varied between countries, depending on the specific conditions in each market and local relationships between banks and retailers.

EFTPOS/debit card innovations in the UK

The development of EFTPOS UK began in 1974 when the Committee of London Clearing Banks (CLCB) approached the Retail Consortium to negotiate the running of the national EFTPOS project. A conflict which undermined the banks' collaborative approach towards a national system, began over competitive bias in the BIS specifications (the Business Inaugural Service, the name for the pilot EFTPOS UK network). There was also a disagreement between Barclays and the other banks over the choice of encryption algorithm for the EFTPOS UK standard, with Barclays threatening to withdraw from EFTPOS UK if its DES[1] algorithm was not chosen. This was seen as significant by the other banks because Barclays owned 300 terminals, part of a network called PDQ (the Barclays proprietary EFTPOS network). Barclays had used the transaction key implementation of the DES algorithm in PDQ. The rival banks' choice of the RSA system for EFTPOS UK would render Barclays' PDQ obsolete (Howells and Hine, 1993, p. 32). After the inauguration of the EFTPOS UK project, members continued to run their own independent card trials such as Counterplus by the Clydesdale Bank, Midland Speedline and NatWest Streamline.

From the bank terminal technology it was a relatively short jump to the UK's first EFTPOS system, Counterplus, again developed through the partnership of Fortronic and the Clydesdale Bank. An acronym for Electronic Funds Transfer at Point of Sale, EFTPOS allows customers to use their banker's card at retail outlets, with payment automatically being transferred from their account to that of the retailer.

In developing the EFTPOS UK system, the main difficulties faced were the security of message encryption and authentication circuits. Since the POS terminal would be sitting on a cashier's desk, there was a requirement for a security system that would produce a message which could not be forged, corrupted, altered or denied and that could be re-verified at a later date.[2] Another challenge for an EFTPOS system was response time, including connect time to dial the central computers. There was a concern that the telephone connection with the banks would not be

Counterplus
Counterplus is the EFTPOS system developed by the Clydesdale Bank in partnership with Fortronic. The Counterplus system allows customers to use their banker's card at retail outlets, with payment automatically being transferred from their current account to that of the retailer.

Midland Speedline
The Speedline point-of-sale computer system was launched by Midland Bank. Midland Speedline has opted for a market share policy, looking for economies of scale and anticipating that EFTPOS usage will develop in a fashion similar to ATMs.

NatWest Streamline
NatWest Streamline is an on-line EFTPOS system launched by the National Westminster Bank. NatWest undertook the Streamline system following an independent EFTPOS trial to compete for cardholders and to acquire retailers.

Innovation process

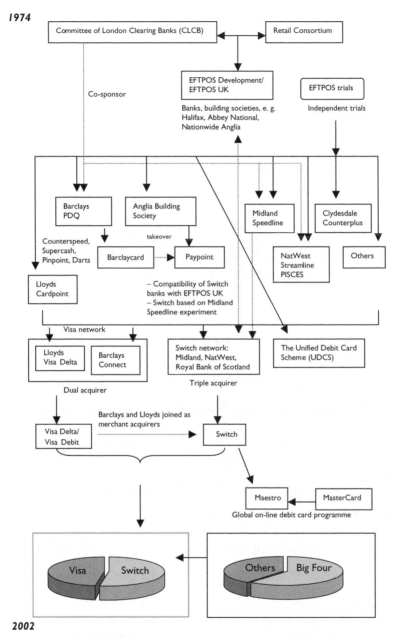

Figure 3.1   The development of the EFTPOS/debit card innovation
Source: The author's design.

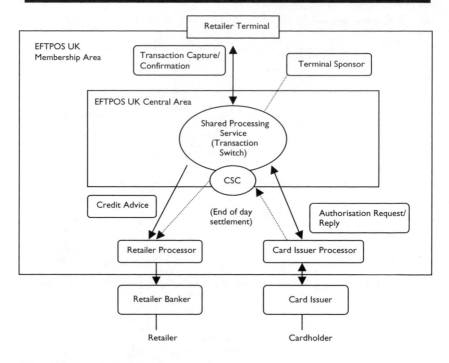

Figure 3.2 EFTPOS UK payment system
Source: Banking World, September 1988, p. 63.

available on a continuous basis, frustrating payment at the cash desks.[3]

Figure 3.2 shows the intended design for the EFTPOS UK payment system. It used IBM System 8 computers running Base 24 software for transaction processing. EFTPOS UK was contracted by British Telecom to develop a telecommunications network to link retailers to the scheme – the ETAN communications system with a backbone X25 Packet Switched Service (PSS) to provide multi-dropping and to warn of network malfunctions.[4]

ETAN
EFTPOS Terminal Access Node (ETAN) is the digital local access telecommunications network set up to link retailer terminals to the scheme, providing a high-quality level of access points and networking performance.

The system was intended to be on-line to prevent fraud. As an encrypted message is sent to the EFTPOS UK processing service, it is directed to the appropriate card issuers' processor for authorisation, who may make a further enquiry to the card issuer. A confirmation message then returns to the terminal along the same route, generating a printed record to be signed. Subject to the usual signature checks, when the transaction is completed, the cardholder's account is debited and the retailer's banking account is automatically credited with the amount of the transaction.[5]

The EFTPOS UK system set-up cost is around £400 million (£150 million for the banks, £150 million for the network suppliers and £100 million for the retailers).[6] To promote the national project, the banks discussed sharing the costs of infrastructure with the retailers. However, the negotiations stalled as retailers criticised the national system as being devised to the advantage of the banks who already had much of the infrastructure for ATM and credit cards in place. The reason for the retailers' resentment of banks was the revelation based on cost-benefit analysis that the banks gained more in financial terms (banks–51.42% of return on investment against the retailers–19.50%) (Howells and Hine, 1993, p. 80; Woodman, 1988, p. 47).

The benefits from the investment of the EFTPOS network arose from the cost advantage when compared to the previous paper-based system. The savings in administration staff, processing centres and security were between 50 percent and 75 percent less than existing paper-based methods (O'Hanlon and Rocha, 1993, p. 34). The transaction cost of EFTPOS is approximately 15 pence compared to the cost of cheque processing of around 50 pence (Howells and Hine, 1991, p. 398).

A genuine form of implementation began in 1987 when Barclays launched its own Visa-branded debit card, Connect. Barclays was the first that decided to go it alone because it saw that it was difficult for EFTPOS UK to obtain unanimous support due to many problems, such as the RSA versus DES argument, PDQ compatibility with the national system and the conflict between the banks and retailers. Thus, Barclays saw that a cooperative approach towards a national EFTPOS system might not work.

Having seen Barclays announce the launch of its own debit card, Lloyds followed by issuing its debit card in the same year

Table 3.1 Benefits, costs, investment and returns for a projected on-line national EFTPOS system in the UK (in millions of pounds)

	Benefit	Customer	Retailer	Banker
(1)	At point of sale	23.52	35.29	—
(2)	Administration	—	15.49	762.56
(3)	Fraud/ bad debt	—	2.32	34.85
(4) = (1)+(2)+(3)	Total benefit	23.52	53.10	797.41
(5)	Running costs	—	18.00	330.00
(6) = (4)-(5)	Net benefit	23.52	35.10	467.40
(7)	Investment	—	180.00	909.00
(8) = (6)/(7)	Return	—	19.50	51.42

Source: Woodman and Diver (1988, p. 5).

RSA

RSA is the public-key algorithm invented by Rivest, Shamir and Adleman. RSA provides digital signatures and therefore helps settle phantom transaction disputes. The algorithm is based upon a one-way hash-function multiplying two large prime numbers. The resulting number serves as the encryption key whereas the deciphering key is based on the two prime numbers. This system is based on the assumption that even very powerful computers take a long time to factor a large figure back into its original primes.

(1987). Barclays and Lloyds' pre-emptive bids undermined collaboration between EFTPOS UK members previously committed to the development of a national system. Midland, NatWest and the Royal Bank of Scotland could not wait until 1989 to have the UDCS[7] in place, and therefore launched their Switch cards in 1988. This resulted in the death of EFTPOS UK: the system only went live for six months and processed just 77,000 transactions.[8]

A rivalry between Lloyds and Barclays, and the Visa banks, on the one hand, and the Switch banks on the other, was established as two different routes emerged to provide an EFTPOS network in the UK.

Switch

The Switch card scheme was the delivery system started by Midland/HSBC, NatWest and the Royal Bank of Scotland in 1988 and joined by other banks and building societies, including

DES (Data Encryption Standard)

DES is the US encryption formula of the Personal Identification Number (PIN). The DES encryption algorithm was developed by IBM in 1976. The encryption algorithm guarantees the integrity of the PIN within the computer system. The PIN is stored in the bank's computers in an encrypted form (as a cipher) for security reasons. The encryption is essential to the functioning of the cards, since it is a means to protect the cardholder from being impersonated by someone who has access to the bank's computer files.

Lloyds TSB, Alliance & Leicester and Halifax as well as other smaller institutions.

Visa Debit (Visa Delta)

Visa Debit is part of the Visa organisation. Visa Debit cards are issued by Barclays, Lloyds TSB and other banks, plus building societies, for use through the LINK network of ATMs.

Most of the members of the Switch network are from the Access (MasterCard) camp in the case of credit cards, and the MINT network in the case of ATM/cash cards, whereas most of the members of the Visa Debit scheme are from the Visa camp in the case of credit cards and the Four Banks network in the case of ATM/cash cards.

The launch of EFTPOS/debit cards involved competition for the recruitment of merchants and their terminals, to capture debit card transactions. Banks competed to support the Switch or Visa networks in order to build competitive relationships with the top 200 retailers, to obtain market share and to gain scale economies in processing over competitors (Garrigan, 1989, p. 14; Howells and Hine, 1993, p. 38). As part of the competition to gain the retailer business, although retailers paid communications costs, their terminals were heavily subsidised by the banks, in contrast with the charging structure of the EFTPOS UK project (table 3.1) which assumed that retailers would pay the full costs of terminals but would not bear a share of communications costs (Howells and Hine, 1993, pp. 82, 236).

Barclays was the innovation pace-setter with its launch of Barclays Connect. Barclays' Visa honour-all-cards rule (requiring all retailers who accept Visa credit cards to accept the Connect card) caused strong resistance among the retailers over Barclays' attempt to charge retailers 2 percent commission (the same percentage rate as for credit cards).[9] Since no free credit period was being provided, retailers refused to accept the card. Barclays was then forced to give in to the retailers' demands by charging a flat rate of 17.5 pence per transaction at the end of 1987.

Table 3.2 shows the major EFTPOS schemes competing to install terminals at retailers' checkout points for debit card acceptance. With regard to the share in the merchant acquirer market

Table 3.2 EFTPOS schemes – number of schemes installed by financial institution

Financial Institution	Scheme	1988		1989		1990	
		Outlets	Terminals	Outlets	Terminals	Outlets	Terminals
Access	Accept	n/a	n/a	3,662	5,562	n/a	n/a
Barclays	PDQ, PIN Point	5,870	3,185	6,218	9,757	12,711	17,551
Clydesdale	Counterplus	64	72	64	72	64	72
Co-operative Bank	Co-op EFTPOS	19	75	25	175	85	373
Funds Transfer Sharing	LINK with BP	23	23	24	24	24	24
Girobank	LINK	2	8	2	8	2	8
Lloyds	Cardpoint	84	58	235	368	2,579	11,742
Midland	Midland Transact	1,076	132	2,650	17,200	10,742	31,089
NatWest	Streamline	2,928	2,440	4,225	8,635	8,750	30,516
Royal Bank of Scotland	Royal Bank EFTPOS	n/a	n/a	295	295	1,050	5,300
Total		10,066	5,993	17,400	42,096	36,007	96,675

Source: Banking World, 1988–1990.

Open system is the shared network of EFTPOS terminals, which enables a member institution and their account holders to obtain access to the benefits offered by electronic payment systems and to keep the expense of deploying the technology reasonable and proportionate to the financial institution's ability to pay (Essinger, 1992). As most card issuers are looking for a way to get more transactions, the open system allows innovators to share EFTPOS terminals with other organisations. Examples of 'open' EFTPOS networks in the UK are Switch and Visa.

(outlets signed), table 3.2 shows that Barclays held the highest share, followed by NatWest and Midland.

Market competition was mainly between banks supporting the Switch scheme and banks supporting the Visa debit card service. Table 3.3 illustrates the growth of debit cards in the UK. Figure 3.3 shows the diffusion of Switch and Visa debit cards. The Switch card scheme was more successful than the Visa card scheme mainly because Switch was developed as an open system and was more practical in terms of offering cheap terminal upgrades to retailers (Essinger, 1992, p. 59, 61). The advent of the duality system (whereby banks could join both networks) in 1988 offered clear benefits to the Switch card scheme. Switch's ability to offer retailers the full acquisition of three different types of card (Switch, Visa, MasterCard) compared to the dual acquiring offered by Visa (Visa, MasterCard) was recognised by the retailers as a clear advantage.

As the Switch card outpaced Visa, Barclays and Lloyds applied to join Switch solely as merchant acquirers. They were turned down because Switch members were Switch card issuers, only some of whom were acquirers. A complaint about the refusal was made by Barclays and Lloyds to the Office of Fair Trading (OFT); their ruling stated that this law was anti-competitive.[10] Switch was finally forced to drop its membership condition in 1990 (Essinger, 1992, p. 62).

Table 3.4 shows the number of EFTPOS/debit cards and current account balances by major financial institution. Figure 3.4 shows that the Big Four clearing banks (Barclays, Lloyds TSB, NatWest, Midland/HSBC) take up the largest share of the debit card market.

In 1992, MasterCard International introduced the Maestro

Table 3.3   The growth of debit cards in the UK

	1989	1990	1992	1995	1996	1997	1998
No. of debit cards ('000)							
Switch	9,159	11,412	12,377	15,162	16,295	18,287	21,791
Visa	4,430	7,540	10,219	13,279	16,178	18,359	20,737
Total	13,589	18,953	22,596	28,441	32,473	36,646	42,529
Increase (%)		39	19	26	14	13	16
No. of transactions (millions)							
Switch	16	71	269	535	684	802	919
Visa	52	121	253	468	587	701	817
Total	68	192	522	1,004	1,270	1,503	1,736
Increase (%)		182	172	92	26	18	16
Value of transactions (£million)							
Switch	483	1,968	6,997	14,971	19,697	23,789	28,199
Visa	1,205	3,163	6,844	13,485	17,358	21,270	25,521
Total	1,688	5,131	13,840	28,456	37,056	45,058	53,720
Increase (%)		204	170	106	30	22	19

Source: APACS Yearbook of Payment Statistics (1995, 1996, 1999).

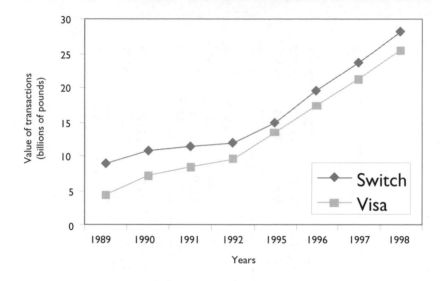

Figure 3.3 Diffusion of debit cards – Switch and Visa
Source: Annual Abstract of Banking Statistics (1993); APACS Plastic Card Review (1999).

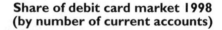

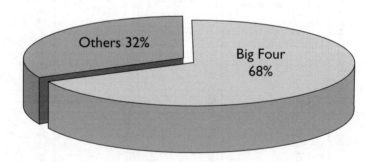

Figure 3.4 Share of debit card market of major banks compared with other industry players
Source: APACS (1999); Key Note Market Report (1999) – Credit & Other Finance Cards.

Table 3.4 The debit card share and current account by major financial institution

	No. of debit cards				Current account balances (£million)				
	1989	1990	1995	1998	1989	1990	1995	1998
Barclays	4,995	5,911	6,765	7,610	10,457	14,604	34,943	41,884
Lloyds TSB	12,175	14,665	13,142	12,660	12,494	16,940	52,504	63,381
NatWest	5,590	5,855	7,311	8,012	19,482	22,271	37,727	45,388
Midland/HSBC	4,931	5,188	5,917	7,093	13,851	19,456	34,551	35,818
Other	7,117	7,810	9,927	22,770	51,579	42,549	96,602	204,829
Total	34,808	39,429	43,062	58,145	107,863	115,820	256,327	391,300

Source: Key Note – Credit & Other Finance Cards (1999, p. 31); Key Note – Personal Banking (1999, p. 39); British Bankers' Association.

global point-of-sale debit network. Midland and NatWest joined Maestro in 1993 to add that international facility[11] to their Switch card scheme.[12] Currently there is growing potential for the wide issuance and use of the online debit cards – Visa Electron and Solo. Online debit cards allow cardholders to pay for goods and services in shops or by mail, telephone and electronic commerce (e-commerce). In the future, e-commerce is expected to be a factor encouraging higher levels of debit card use. The e-commerce initiatives in card innovations are led by Marbles, Goldfish, Capital One, Egg, etc.

COMPETITION IN THE DEBIT CARD MARKET

Figure 3.5 shows how the progress of innovation was shaped by innovators' (banks and building societies) strategy. The outer circles represent the total revenue pool resulting from the innovation. The inner circles represent the size of the market share of individual innovators in the retailer–acquirer business. In the

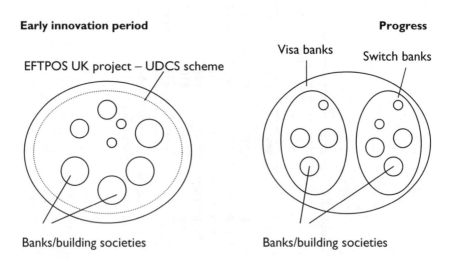

Figure 3.5 The progress of innovation in the context of innovators' strategy – EFTPOS/debit cards

early innovation period, banks and building societies competed to launch their own EFTPOS schemes while joining the national project, EFTPOS UK. Under a proprietary EFTPOS service, the scope of service (the internal benefits) was limited, since the cards could only be used at the dedicated points of sale. After the failure of the national project, banks and building societies opted to join the Switch and Visa Debit schemes. The banks and building societies could then realize increased benefits in terms of the extended scope of debit card usage (external benefits) from the integration of the network of retail outlets.

Competition in offering fund transfers under a debit payment scheme began in the 1980s. While innovators (banks and building societies) participated in EFTPOS UK to develop the national system, they also pursued a competitive strategy by running their own proprietary EFTPOS trials (figure 3.1). Innovators provided the EFTPOS services to improve the quality as well as the efficiency of service products (EFTPOS provides funds transfer at the point of sale instead of withdrawing money from ATMs to make purchases in cash). Innovators probably realized that they were not able to achieve competitive advantage through competitive customer acquisition because of the current account link. The tying of EFTPOS/debit cards to the current accounts made it difficult for banks to extend their market share in debit payments beyond the market share of bank accounts.

Barclays' first move in its strategy towards the launch of EFTPOS/debit cards was a logical way of leveraging its large share in the credit card market with extensive merchant contacts. Barclays saw no reason to submit to other EFTPOS UK members when this might reduce its own opportunities to win a substantial market share by being the first bank to have an independent debit card sheme. In other words, Barclays believed that its strong position in the credit card business would provide an advantage in launching its debit card. However, this was an overestimation. The use of Visa's honour-all-cards rule, forcing retailers who accept Visa to accept Connect cards, undermined Barclays' ability to exploit first-mover advantage; major retailers refused to accept the expensive Barclays' Connect card.

Midland/HSBC aimed to gain a share in the merchant–acquirer business by offering cheap terminals to build up good relations with retailers. Midland's attempt to control a delivery system can be seen from its largest share of terminals signed in the years 1989 and 1990 (table 3.2). However, Midland also failed to gain any competitive advantage from its venture. Its share in the merchant–acquirer market (outlets signed) in 1990 (30%) was still less than Barclays' share (35%) even though Barclays had suffered from the loss of its previous market share. Midland's share was not much better, even, than NatWest's (24%).

The Switch and Visa Debit networks eventually became open systems. As an open system, this gave benefits to the participating players in terms of a networked distribution (network of retail outlets) which allowed debit cards to grow widely (figure 3.3). This open system helped small banks to launch their own debit card schemes and increase market share by using the resources and networks of industry competitors. Other advantages included the scale-based benefits in terms of cost-saving from the use of electronic processing (electronic fund transfer) to replace cheque processing (paper fund transfer).

However, although the open system gave benefits to all participating players, no one gained a significant competitive advantage from the merchant acquisition. The current account base, whereby the innovator could cross-sell other banking products and generate revenues, was common among innovators. It is perhaps true to claim that EFTPOS/debit cards were simply a money transmission facility which enabled the cardholders to obtain cash and pay for goods and services (an additional facility for ATM/cash cards).

SUMMARY

The complexity of the EFTPOS system lies in its compatibility requirement of the electronic interface among multi-parties – consumer/bank card, the retailer terminal, telephone switching and the bank clearing system. EFTPOS UK, an underlying wide collaborative approach, failed with the reason given from the interview that the national EFTPOS system team were trying to build a Rolls-Royce solution but in fact all the banks needed was a very simple card which would back into their existing system. In this respect, it was perceived that all the participating banks knew that it was the wrong solution but all (except Barclays) were reluctant to opt out for strategic reasons. As a result, the EFTPOS UK solution was clearly going nowhere. Although the participating banks invested in the centralised system, none of them relinquished their intention to develop their own system.

Later, Switch and Visa Debit were developed as the two major systems competing to launch their card schemes using compatible technology (standard-setting for hardware and software for interoperability among the retailers and financial institutions and for transactions clearing). Collaboration in terms of merchant relationships is required in order to gain access to the retailer's terminals for the acceptance of debit card schemes. Cooperative competition can be seen from the banks competing to subsidise terminals to the retailer to get into the retailer's business. The competition then came to be seen as banks supporting the Switch scheme and banks supporting a Visa debit card service. The benefits of collaboration are in terms of a networked distribution (network of retail outlets), which enables debit cards to grow widely. With regard to the small banks, the open system of Switch and Visa Debit helps them to launch their debit card schemes and enhance their market share by using the resources and network of their competitors, rather than being isolated banks within the industry itself.

By nature, the EFTPOS/debit card innovation has complexity in terms of product differentiation. The debit card was a service expansion from the credit fund transfer (credit card) to include the debit fund transfer at the point of sale. Any feature offerings, such as the cashback scheme, could easily be replicated by the other innovators. Therefore, innovators competed to increase the number of locations of card acceptance in order to enable customers to access direct debit facilities internationally. This particular form of collaboration reflects an innovator's attempt to lead the field in electronic banking and to establish brand loyalty with the expanded scope of service, e.g. Midland/HSBC and NatWest's connection of their EFTPOS network with Maestro.

The analysis of the EFTPOS/debit card evolution has shown that, while the banks and building societies participated in EFTPOS UK to develop the national system, they also pursued competitive strategy by running proprietary EFTPOS trials. This is because the innovators saw more benefits of being the market leader in the EFTPOS/debit card market. Concerning Barclays' first-mover strategy in going alone, the launch of its EFTPOS/debit card was unsuccessful because of the bank's over-estimation of achievement in the credit card market. Barclays paid high marketing costs but could not establish a good relation-ship with customers. The 'honour all cards rule' was the wrong strategy and undermined its ability to have the first-mover advantage. Thus, Barclays failed to extend its competitive posi-tion from the credit card business into the debit card business despite pursuing the first-mover strategy.

The EFTPOS/debit card innovation, by itself, did not create the new customer base (since it was based on existing current account customers)[13] that would enable innovators to launch new prod-ucts or enter new businesses successfully. Furthermore, the use of the current account customer base by the bank to cross-sell further financial products seemed to be common among innova-tors (card issuers). Hence, there was no indication that any innovator gained a superior advantage in the case of the EFTPOS/debit card.

CHAPTER 4

Competition, Innovation and Performance: The Evolution of the Bank Card Business

The studies of ATM/cash cards, credit cards and EFTPOS/debit cards demonstrate that these cards have been widely adopted. Figure 4.1 shows the evolution of card innovations. The process of innovation corresponds to Rothwell's Systems Integration and Networking (SIN) model. This move has been characterised by a shift away from the concept of 'Technology Push' towards 'Networking Structure'. Through a system of collaboration, the progression of card innovations is elevated from the firm, or regional, level to cross the boundaries of the industry level, towards a national or even a global level.

> **Rothwell's Systems Integration and Networking (SIN) model**
> Rothwell proposed five generations of innovation models to explain the historic pattern of innovation. The networking model (Rothwell, 1992) is presented as a response to avoid the failure of innovation, particularly in commercialisation. The generations of innovation represent an evolution of innovation from a competitive to a collaborative structure.

Table 4.1 Rothwell's model on the patterns of innovation

Generation	Key features
First	Technology push: simple linear sequential process
Second	Need pull: simple linear sequential process
Third	Coupling model: recognising interaction between different elements and feedback loops between them
Fourth	Integrated mode: integration within the firm, upstream with key suppliers and downstream with demanding and active customers, emphasis on linkages and alliances
Fifth	Systems integration and extensive networking model: flexible and customized response, continuous innovation

Source: Rothwell (1992a).

Technology Push

The technology push concept is focused around the elements of the technology supply industry bank card manufacturers, EFTPOS and ATM system manufacturers.

Level of progression

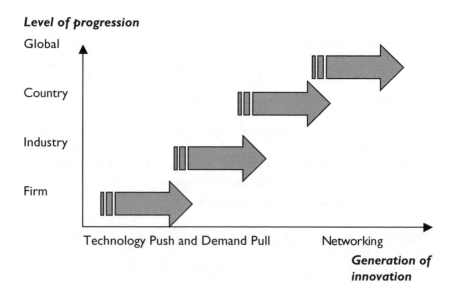

Figure 4.1 Progression of innovation
Source: The author's design, based on Rothwell (1992, 1992a) and Utterback and Abernathy (1975).

Partial external benefits are the partial benefits from an inter-connected network of ATMs. Through collaboration, the card issuers could share the development costs with non-competing collaborators and provide their customers with remote service without themselves having to achieve national or international networks of ATMs. For example, the ATM networks of Mint (Midland, NatWest, TSB, Clydesdale and Northern banks); Four Banks (Barclays, Lloyds, Royal Bank of Scotland and Bank of Scotland) and LINK (35 financial institutions, including Abbey National, Girobank and Co-operative Bank as well as building societies) enable cardholders to access any ATMs within the pooled ATM network.

Figure 4.2 shows the progress of adoption of bank cards in the bank card business. Theoretically, the figure also demonstrates that card-based services could be provided on an individual, bank-by-bank basis. In practice, innovators saw the advantage of entering into collaboration to provide the service on an extended scope basis, branching out beyond the limited scope of their own markets via a low-cost, low-investment joint card scheme venture. Also, the extended scope of card usage can be regarded as a great benefit to customers whose accessibility to banking services is highly improved. For example, when innovators linked up their proprietary ATM networks to form interconnected networks such as Four Banks and LINK, the cards of one institution can be used at ATMs maintained by all of the network members (this is known as partial external benefits). As these interconnected networks melted into LINK, and joined other international networks such as Visa Plus and MasterCard Cirrus, a single, local institution's card could be used at ATMs world-wide (known as full external benefits). As innovators entered into

Full external benefits are the full benefits from an inter-connected network of ATMs. An open international ATM network allows maximum potential diffusion for the ATM/cash card innovation since card issuers' customers can use their bank card at any other ATM. The sharing of ATM facilities between financial institutions and networks in different countries increases direct access for the customers through a network of bank ATMs.

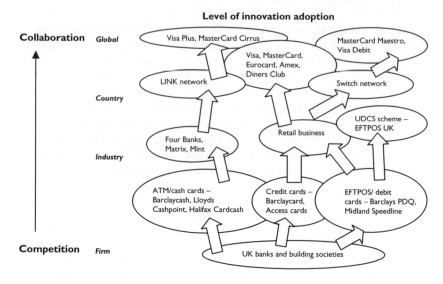

Figure 4.2 The progress of card innovations
Source: The author's design.

collaboration, they began to enjoy benefits (in terms of the scope of card usage) beyond those that any individual innovator could internalise.

Figure 4.3 shows the payment volumes of debit cards, credit cards and cheques in the UK. Use of the former grew largely at the expense of the paper-based payment system. Paper-based payment transactions (volume) have fallen by 21 percent over the last 10 years (1988–98), whereas card payments have increased over threefold since 1988 and now account for 44 percent of all non-cash payments. Payment by debit cards bypassed all types of non-cash payments, accounting for 59 percent of all plastic card purchases. In 1998, the number of debit cards in issue in the UK was 42.5 million, a more than 100 percent increase from 1991, whereas the credit cards (Visa and MasterCard) only achieved a 44 percent increase.[1]

Figures 4.4–4.6 show the financial performance of major players in the card market in various contexts. Generally, the Big Four perform better than other industry players in financial terms, taking a market share of over 50 percent, which explains their ability to provide card-based services on an extended basis

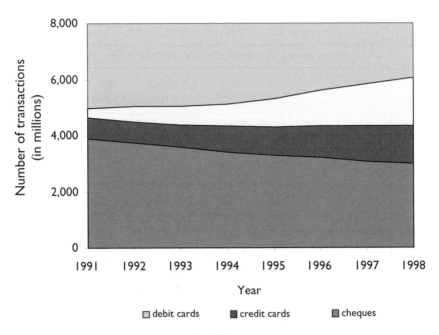

Figure 4.3 Payment volumes in the UK
Source: APACS Yearbook of Payment Statistics (1999).

(the Big Four own the largest fleet of ATMs in the country and have the largest number of issuers and acquirers for credit cards and EFTPOS/debit cards). The number of branches of the Big Four banks account for about two-thirds of the total number of branches in the banking sector. By getting increased access to customers, the possibility of having access to customer information, which will enable the banks to use that information to launch more competitive products, becomes a reality. According to a review of UK banking services conducted by Don Cruickshank in 2000, consumers tended to choose the nearest bank when it came to purchasing banking products.

In terms of the overall patterns and picture in the market competition of ATM/cash cards, credit cards and EFTPOS/debit cards, the ability to achieve competitive advantage is crucial to understanding market forces. This ability is based, in part, on the nature of innovation. It can also be argued that the ability to achieve competitive advantage is associated with the nature of customer hold.[2] The nature of low customer hold in the case of

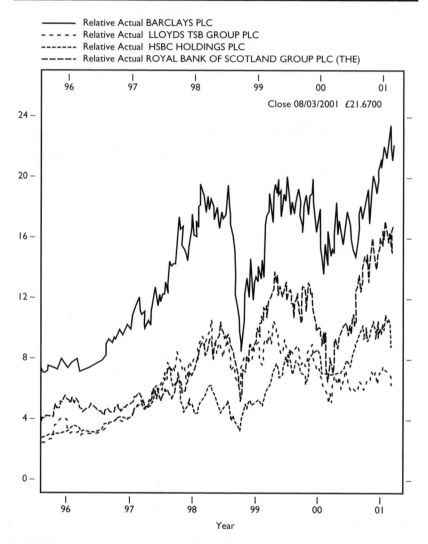

Figure 4.4 The share price of major players in the card market
Source: Sequencer.

credit cards gives innovators the opportunity to maximise internal benefits. The potential benefits from exploiting the innovation are high relative to the total benefits. However, when the nature of the innovation is of a high/strong customer hold (as in the case of ATM/cash cards and EFTPOS/debit cards), then innovators tend to collaborate. This is because they see that collaboration would

Return on equity (%)

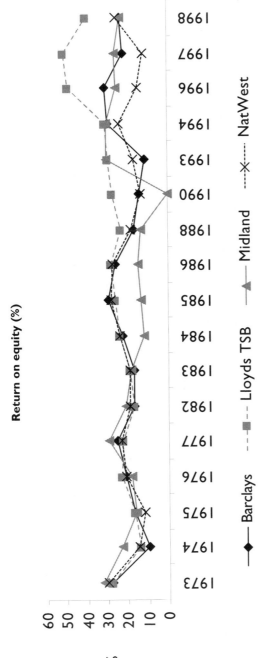

Figure 4.5 The financial performance of major players in the card market (as set out on pp. 63–6)
Source: APACS (1999), Cruickshank (2000), Sequencer, Lehman Brothers, February 1999.

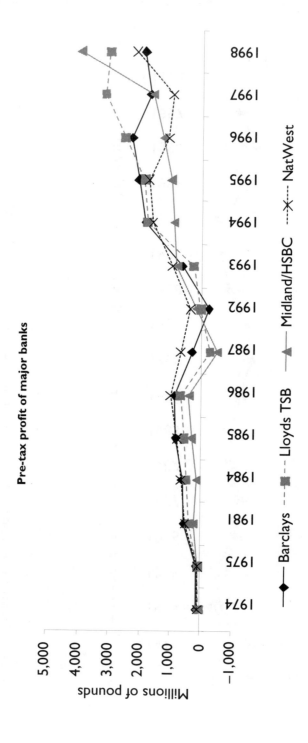

Pre-tax profit of major banks

Millions of pounds

—◆— Barclays   ---■--- Lloyds TSB
—◆— Midland/HSBC   ---✕--- NatWest

5,000
4,000
3,000
2,000
1,000
0
-1,000

1974 1975 1981 1984 1985 1986 1987 1992 1993 1994 1995 1996 1997 1998

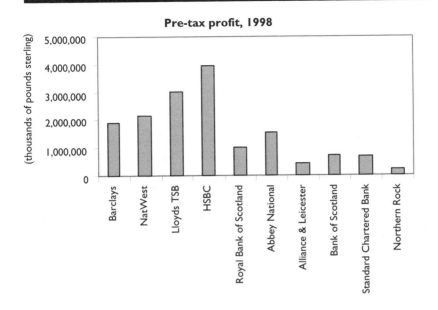

Pre-tax profit, 1998

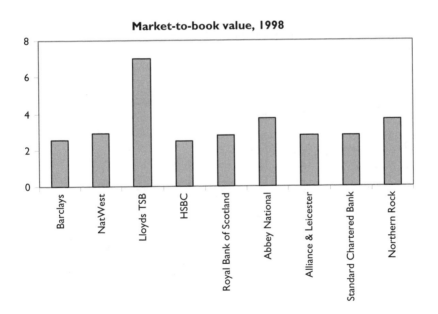

Market-to-book value, 1998

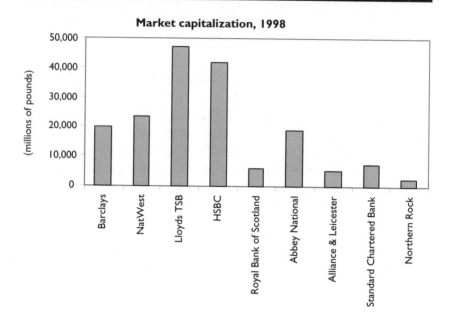

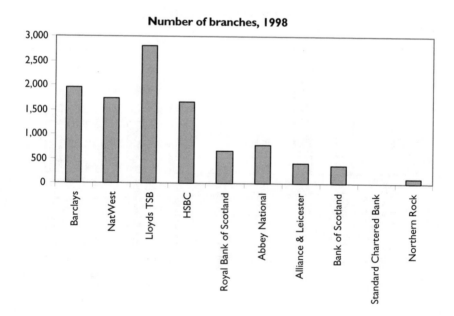

Note: The number of branches of Standard Chartered Bank is very small, and does not register on the graph.

1. Turnover (sales, in thousands of pounds sterling)

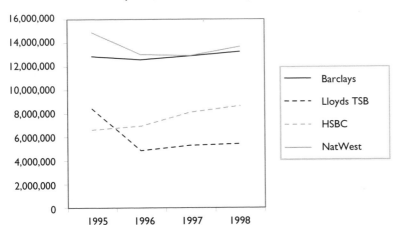

2. Operating profit (in thousands of pounds sterling)

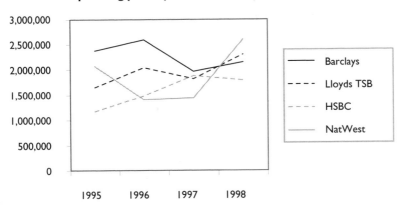

Figure 4.6 Financial performance of the Big Four banks in the UK, currency in pounds (as set out on pp. 67–70)

Source: Key Note Market Report: Credit and Other Finance Cards (1999), Personal Banking (1999).

3. Pretax profit (in thousands of pounds sterling)

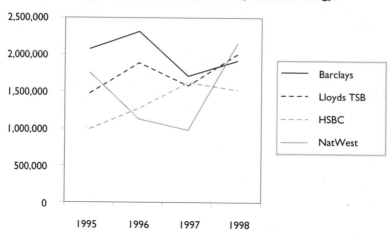

4. Profit margin (in percentages)

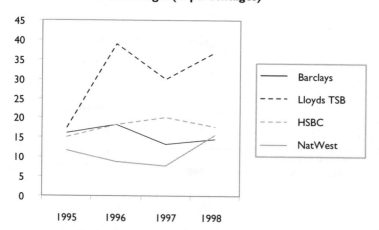

5. No. of employees

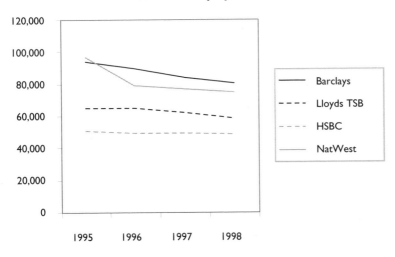

6. Sales per employee

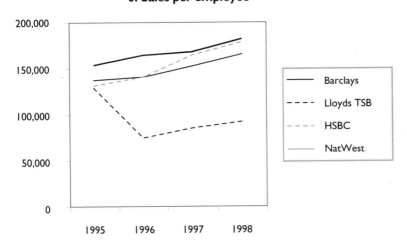

7. Profit per employee

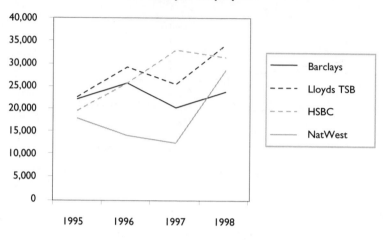

8. Number of branches

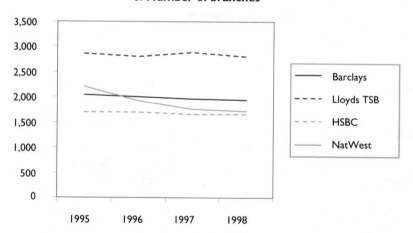

Internal benefits are the benefits from pursuing a going-it-alone strategy. For example, Barclays saw the use of first-mover strategy in launching the credit card as an opportunity to build up the customer base, market share and establish the brand status. The internal benefits can be seen from Barclaycard's highest market share in the UK in the 1960s and 1970s. Barclaycard could also remain the market share leader in the credit card market in the 1980s and 1990s despite the attack by competitors.

pose few threats to their existing customer base. By adopting a collaborative strategy, banks can lower investment costs and improve their customer service network. A policy of non-collaboration would result in the bank being excluded from benefits enjoyed by their collaborative competitors.

The chosen strategies adopted for each bank card depend on the expected benefits. If external benefits are large relative to total benefits, innovators tend to use a collaborative strategy. In the early stages of market development, three bank card innovations competed to provide services on an individual basis. As domestic and international mobility and availability were low, external benefits lost through non-collaboration were also low. However, when the innovations evolved and reached the stage of commercialisation, the launch of cards for market competition, both domestic and international mobility and availability increased.

Expected benefits are the benefits in terms of gaining greater access to the new market. Alliances with strategic partners enable the card issuers to extend the scope of service by combining the delivery channels of others. The expected benefits also include the ability to launch new products/services or enter new businesses.

External benefits are the benefits from orchestrating partners' capabilities that can only be obtained through collaboration. External benefits can be seen in terms of more options to provide new products or more value-added services that satisfy customers. For example, the combination of Barclays' payment functions with BT Cellnet's telecommunications capabilities enables Barclays to offer a value-added digital mobile banking service.

Since the external benefits, as part of the total innovation benefits, increased (figure 4.2), these benefits became attractive to
innovators, and thus they tended to enter into collaboration.

With shifts in the internal/external benefit position and
changes in the strength of customer hold, market strategies tend
to transform during the process of innovation. The change from
competitive strategy to collaborative strategy in the case of
Barclaycard provides a good example: Barclaycard joined the
Visa network to lessen the impact of its undermined competitive
position and to enjoy the benefits, such as the extended scope of
service, that collaboration provided. Barclaycard could not afford
to put itself at a scope disadvantage relative to its competitors
since this would further erode its position in the credit card
market.

The analysis of three cases of card innovations shows that
innovators finally entered into collaboration as a means of
accessing benefits from the innovation that were previously
unavailable. The use of collaboration saw the innovation develop
into an open system. For example, LINK (in the case of
ATM/cash cards); Visa and MasterCard, in the case of credit
cards; and Switch and Visa Debit in the case of EFTPOS/debit
cards. The use of collaboration also helped reduce the cost of
investment in reaching maximum diffusion on a competitive
basis by facilitating idea-sharing among innovators.

Innovation management is critical to the success or failure of
the bank card. Since rival innovators could purchase the newest
technology in the third-party market, the timing of the innovation release is important. Also, there are no means of protecting
a proprietary advantage through patent laws in any of the cases
of card innovation. The importance of timing to the market plan
can be seen in the case of Barclaycard, which gained the highest
market share in credit cards from its first-mover strategy.
However, adopting a first-mover strategy will not always establish a competitive advantage. Barclays did not have a competitive
advantage in the case of ATM/cash cards and EFTPOS/debit
cards despite being the first mover. This is mainly because the
EFTPOS/debit card accounts are generally tied to current
accounts. In other words, customers owning EFTPOS/debit
cards generally own a current account. Thereby, the nature of
strong customer hold makes any banks launching new

ATM/cash cards or EFTPOS/debit cards face difficulties in stealing customers from existing banks. The different outcomes from the pursuit of the same strategy demonstrate the sensitivity of the innovation process to industry structure and the significance of internal versus external benefits at any time.

Competitive advantage established before the open system stage can be maintained but only if the innovator continues to upgrade its card capabilities, even as rival cards are released. Collaboration is, therefore, less expensive than investment by a single innovator, and makes it less difficult to reach a wide customer base. Barclaycard was able to launch successive card innovations, because its large customer base, built during the competitive era, provided a market advantage.

SUMMARY

"We're a great partner to work with because we both will make money. It's not because of partnership – it's because of customer relationships."

(Marc Andreessen, Netscape,
in Cusumano and Yoffie, 1998, p. 81)

The three bank card innovations (ATM/cash cards, credit cards, EFTPOS/debit cards) represent the adoption of technology in the financial services industry in new ways. ATM/cash cards represent the concept of self-service banking by using ATM technology to bypass the branch. Credit cards implement the concept of a self-service loan where the credit funds transfer is initiated off of the bank premises (the point of sale). EFTPOS/debit cards represent an extension of fund transfer from the location of the account (bank branch) to the point of sale.

The state of development of the three card innovations initially began with competition and progressed to collaboration. The case of ATM/cash cards began with a proprietary network (e.g. Barclays' BarclayCash/BarclayBank, Lloyds' Cashpoint, Halifax's Cardcash) and gradually developed over time to an integrated network (e.g. Four Banks, Mint, Matrix, LINK). The case of credit cards initially began with competition to issue exclusively with Visa or MasterCard among the card-issuing banks and subsequently moved towards the dual system. The case of EFTPOS represented the first attempt at 1–to–1 competition between bank and retailer and moved towards more cooperation between banking institutions and retail consortiums.

The case studies of ATM/cash cards, credit cards and EFTPOS/debit cards have shown that the complexity of card innovations generally came from the pressures of market competition. Innovators in the card business faced market complexity as the product differentiation of card innovations was not strong. The lack of patent protection meant that the card innovations seemed to be standardised in the whole industry and the customers could always find alternative suppliers. Moreover, as the innovation became an open system, this allowed increasing competition. The banks' new competitors had an advantage in that they did not have to concern a capital investment requirement. As a result, this engendered more complexity in competition from the appearance of new competitors and new substitute products.

In market competition, innovators, in the case of ATM/cash cards, credit cards and EFTPOS/debit cards, could launch the cards on an individual basis. However, innovators chose to adopt a collaborative strategy to improve competitiveness and avoid being at a competitive disadvantage. The use of the collaborative strategy was also to create a service quality advantage; for example, Barclays and BT Cellnet or NatWest and Orange in mobile banking to allow redemption of phone minutes. Innovators stated that they would collaborate only with those who could add value to their own brand, as one banker remarked: 'We look for a win–win strategy and only choose partners with similar strategic goals to ourselves . . . if we have to collaborate, we have to make sure we can improve our position, get a good return and enhance our brand.'

From the analysis, the process of innovation involves two types of collaboration: horizontal collaboration and vertical collaboration.

Horizontal collaboration

Horizontal collaboration refers to collaboration with the competitors in the industry in which the innovators operate. There can be levels of collaboration within horizontal collaboration: collaboration within the industry in the UK and collaboration within the industry outside the UK.

Vertical collaboration

Vertical collaboration refers to collaboration with non-competitors outside the area in which the innovators operate. Collaboration with the retailer business for credit and debit card usage in the case of credit cards and EFTPOS/debit cards, provides an example of this type of collaboration. The aim of the innovators in using vertical collaboration is to maintain and increase their market share by offering product differentiation to increase customer satisfaction, improve customer loyalty and gain new customers in their marketplace.

The strategic analysis has shown that being first to the market could help achieve competitive advantage and this is clearly demonstrated in the case of Barclays' Barclaycard. However, this was not the case for ATM/cash cards and EFTPOS/debit cards, although Barclays was also the first mover in these instances. The competitive advantage was not apparent as the off-line BarclayCash was overtaken by superior on-line technology within a few years. Its unfavourable charging structure (in the case of EFTPOS/debit cards) also led to customer alienation.

In the case of ATM/cash cards, credit cards and EFTPOS/debit cards, the issues regarding the innovation process and innovators' strategies are: (1) how to compete successfully; (2) how advantage over competitors can be achieved; (3) what strategies do innovators take into account during the innovation process; and (4) why a particular strategy is adopted over others. These aspects of innovation management help to build a basis for understanding the innovation process of smart cards discussed in chapter 5.

Smart Cards

This chapter presents the case history as well as an analysis of the smart card innovation. The innovation in smart cards is continuing to develop all the time; to ensure that the most up-to-date information on smart cards is utilised, this chapter draws on primary source materials. The analysis of smart cards is based on perspectives drawn from the Smart Card 2000 conference in London, and through interviews and a questionnaire survey. This chapter focuses, in particular, on the importance of multi-party inter-dependence in commercialising the smart card innovation.

HISTORY OF THE SMART CARD

Smart cards are plastic cards which can, like the magnetic stripe, store data, albeit megabytes rather than bytes. Where they really differ, however, is that smart cards contain a microprocessor – a miniature computer that can manipulate, update and control access to data, perform calculations and support digital interfaces such as wired and wireless telecom and computer networks (Bright, 1988, p. 33; Proton World Fact Sheet – Smart Card). They also have the ability to interchange data with external communi-

Digital certificates

Digital certificates are issued by a trusted issuing authority. They are digital documents attesting to the binding of a public key to an individual or entity. They allow verification of the claim that a given public key belongs to a given individual or entity. In the e-commerce environment, the Secure Electronic Transaction (SET) protocol specifies a method of entity authentication by exchanging digital certificates. The verification of cardholder and merchant validity is done by validating the digital signatures of the

cators – ATMs, telephones or readers. The capacity of the chip is large enough to support multiple applications and house a variety of identification and security tools, such as digital certificates for safeguarding Internet transactions and biometric identification.

The smart card innovation reflects a technological substitution for ageing magnetic stripes. It is important to realise that the two technologies, magnetic and smart, are not independent, and thus the process of substituting the former technology will not be straightforward. In other words, the pattern of smart card diffusion appears to be a parallel substitution of technology.[1] The smart card technology has not taken over the existing magnetic stripe card technology. This is because at present both technologies are used at the same time; for example, ATM/cash cards using magnetic stripe card technology as well as smart card technology.

Table 5.1 shows the technical parameters of magnetic stripe card technology in comparison with smart card technology.

Figure 5.1 (upper figure) represents the adoption of bank card

Biometrics

Biometric technology is a method of authentication. It measures human characteristics such as voice, fingerprint and iris pattern and thus eliminates the problems associated with password management. Biometric technology provides an additional security layer to the smart card system. Biometric module capabilities are embedded in the smart card chip to verify users' authenticity for a secure access control system. Biometrics usually work by comparing the presented identity with a template (typically 1,000 bytes), stored either on a database, smart card or optical card.

Table 5.1 Comparison of technical parameters – magnetic stripe and smart card technology

	Magnetic stripe technology	Smart card technology
Functionality	Mono-functionality	Multi-functionality
Memory capacity	• 140 characters • Limited storage capacity and hence can only be used with a single application	• 8-bit/16-bit/32-bit micro-processors • Increased storage capacity to support multiple applications on one card
Infrastructure and processing	• Very high network and central processor costs for on-line real-time verification • Requires transactions clearing and settlement for users	• Off-line readers with information about transactions downloadable after the transaction at a lower cost • No requirement of a third party to settle and clear transactions
Programmability	• Not programmable • No reloadable value	• Can be programmed to support complex, memory intensive products • Allows for reloadable value
Security	• Visual inspection of signature, PIN verification, on-line verification • Less secure, open to fraud	• Digital signatures, encryption, digitized photographs, retina scans, fingerprints, etc. • More secure, lower fraud loss

Source: Summarised from Bright (1988), Brown and Brown (1987), Gandy (1999), Kaplan (1995).

innovations using magnetic stripe technology and smart card technology.[2] Credit cards, ATM/cash cards and EFTPOS/debit cards have traditionally used plastic cards with a magnetic stripe since the 1970s. Whereas these cards have reached a level of wide adoption, the launch of bank cards using smart card technology has only just begun. The future of the smart card as trend A, B or C (figure 5.1 lower figure) depends on the extent to which innovators (players) in the smart card industry see collaboration as a means to exploit smart card technology.

Although smart cards have many applications and possibilities, this book focuses on smart cards incorporating financial

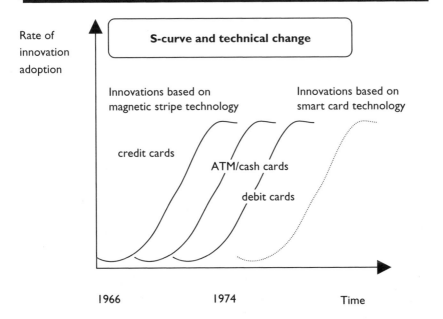

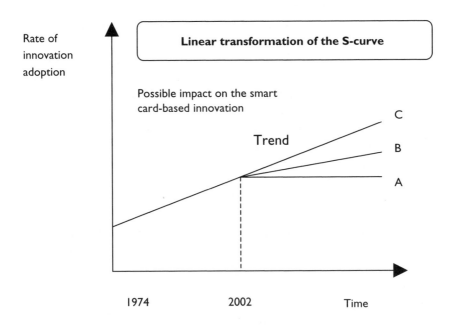

Figure 5.1   The potential adoption of smart cards

applications. A smart card for financial applications is a card which provides payment functionalities such as debits/credits and e-cash (for use as an alternative to paper notes and coins). Smart cards for financial applications will include:

1. The specialist card for financial applications.
2. The multi-purpose card, combining the functionalities of financial applications with non-financial applications such as loyalty schemes, transport cards, SIM cards, etc.

The reason to look at smart cards for financial applications is because many industry analysts see the future of smart cards as a combination of financial and non-financial applications. Smart cards for financial applications also involve many of the issues explored in the case studies of the bank card business in chapters 1–3. By focussing on smart cards for financial applications, insights into previous card innovations will provide some guidelines for the diffusion of smart cards.

Given the capabilities of smart cards, it is perhaps surprising that their history can be traced as far back as 1968 when plastic cards, as carriers of microchips, were first developed by the German inventors Jürgen Dethloff and Helmut Rötrupp. Two years later, in 1970, Kunitaka Arimura made a similar break-through. However, the first practical move came with Roland Moreno's smart card patent in France in 1974 that incorporated a programmable integrated circuit within the bank card. Moreno registered the patent on behalf of the company Innovatron. HoneywellBull was the first company to apply for a license from Innovatron in 1976, followed by Flonic Schlumberger in 1979 and Philips in 1981 (Bright, 1988, p. 22).

In the nascent development of smart card technology, these three companies (HoneywellBull, Schlumberger and Philips) faced substantial technical difficulties in incorporating a micro-processor, memory and other components into a single chip. When the early smart card equipped with microprocessor was developed, it was somewhat thicker than ISO standards, and thus was dubbed the 'fat card'. To solve the problem of data capacity, HoneywellBull chose a Motorola microprocessor, while Philips opted for an Intel microprocessor. The formidable challenge of smart card technology in the 1970s was how to develop

Smart card technology

Applications

- Smart debit card
- Smart credit card
- E-cash
- Smart card for mobile phone
- Smart loyalty card
- Smart card for transport
- Smart telephone card
- Smart card for Pay TV

Smart cards – financial applications

Specialist Cards
- Smart debit card
- Smart credit card
- E-cash

Multipurpose Cards
- The card which has the main functionality of banking applications interacting with non-banking applications such as loyalty schemes, transport card, mobile SIM card, etc.

Smart cards – non-financial applications

- Smart card for mobile phone
- Smart loyalty card
- Smart card for transport
- Smart telephone card
- Smart card for Pay TV

Figure 5.2 The applications of smart card technology

Innovation process

1970

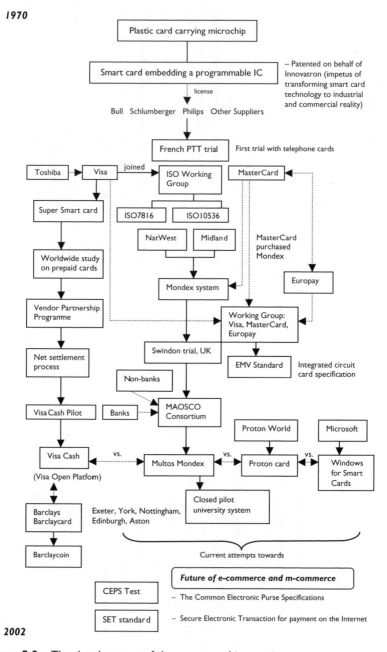

Figure 5.3 The development of the smart card innovation
Source: The author's design.

PROM (Programmable Read Only Memory) is a memory chip on which data can be written only once. PROM retains the data contents when the computer is turned off.

EPROM (Erasable Programmable Read Only Memory) is a special type of PROM that can be erased by exposing it to ultraviolet light. The light clears its contents, making it possible to reprogram the memory.

EEPROM (Electrically-Erasable Programmable Read Only Memory) is similar to a PROM, but requires only electricity to be erased. EEPROM allows smart card applications involving frequent usage and high memory consumption rate to be developed.

reprogrammability since electrically-erasable PROM (EEPROM) technology was itself still being developed and was expensive. The thickness problem was finally solved in 1981 with the ISO standard thickness of 0.76 mm, and with monochip construction. The monochip allowed the smart card to be used in existing ATMs and other magnetic card readers and so it could be offered to the banking industry as a hybrid card (Bright, 1988, pp. 23–4).

The first smart card field trial was successfully carried out by the French PTT (Postal and Telecommunications Services) with telephone cards in 1984. Deutsche Telecom followed the French, with telephone card trials three years later. However, the progress of smart cards in the financial industry as bank cards was slow due to the complexity and the existing infrastructure of the banking systems. The difficulties include the creation of communications protocols, and security lines for facilitating interchanges of electronic payment transactions.

A major advance in the financial sector occured in 1984 when Visa and MasterCard began planning a payment system using a chip card. In 1988 Visa tested the world's first multi-function chip card, called the SuperSmart card, in Japan. This experiment allowed Visa to test technical aspects of the technology and evaluate the acceptability of services among consumers. In 1990, Visa undertook further research on prepaid cards to understand

Standard Committee 17
Standard Committee 17 is the ISO Standard Committee developing standards for identification cards and related devices. The key working groups are WG1 (Mag Stripe Cards and Test Methods), WG4 (Contact Chip Cards) and WG8 (Contactless Chip Cards).

Technical Committee 68
The ISO Technical Committee 68 (TC68) is the committee developing international technical standards in the financial services industry, including banking and securities. The ISO TC68 was formed in 1948. The United States is the secretariat of ISO/TC68.

Contact
The cards with contact nature refer to the cards accommodating integrated circuits with electrical contacts. These contacts are listed as C1 through C8. The interaction between the cards and the readers is made through the contact pad.

Contactless integrated circuit cards
The contactless cards allow cardholders to tap or wave their cards on an equipped merchant terminal for transmitting payment details on-line. The use of contactless cards eliminates the need to swipe the card through a reader.

worldwide developments of prepaid card systems and stored value products (Kaplan, 1995, pp. 182–3).

In terms of the development of card and industry standards, the major group responsible for such decisions was the International Standards Organisation (ISO), with two working groups developing chip card standards – Standard Committee 17 and Technical Committee 68. Among the most commonly referenced ISO smart card standards are ISO 7816 (integrated circuit cards with contact nature) and ISO 10536 (contactless integrated circuit cards) (Kaplan, 1995, pp. 210–12).

E-CASH

Applying smart card technology to the concept of electronic cash (e-cash) began in 1990 with the Mondex card, an e-cash application developed by the National Westminster Bank in the UK. In 1993, Midland Bank joined the project as the second banking partner in a 50:50 equity partnership. The Swindon experiment, the first Mondex pilot experiment, was launched in July 1995, followed by many international trials. The first city-wide Mondex pilot was in Guelph in Ontario, Canada. The project ran from September 1996 to October 1998 and involved a number of Canadian deposit-taking financial institutions. The significance of the project was that Guelph was the most comprehensive implementation of an electronic cash system anywhere in the world. The operation of full electronic cash currency involved merchants, payphones and vending machines, along with services such as taxis, buses, home deliveries and street vendors. Consumers also used Mondex cards in everyday activities. Mondex planned to use the Guelph project as a blueprint for its global roll-out.[3] Another important pilot offering the prospect of inter-operability began in 1997 when MasterCard and Visa launched a pilot program involving both Mondex and Visa Cash in the Upper West Side of Manhattan. The pilot provided merchants with a single terminal to process both Mondex and Visa Cash transactions. Of equal importance, Mondex has managed to sell franchises to financial service companies across the world[4] (Bank for International Settlements, 2000, pp. 12, 101; Gandy, 1999, p. 76; Vartanian, 1998, p. 483).

A major competitor to Mondex, Visa International launched the smart card scheme Visa Cash in 1995. Visa's own electronic

The Swindon experiment was the smart card pilot experiment of Mondex system. The trials on various payment applications were run in the Swindon area of the UK in 1995. The Mondex trials accorded momentum to the innovation as it was a real attempt by Mondex to set an industry standard for the UK by taking the technological lead. Mondex works like an electronic wallet and has the capacity to carry several currencies.

purse 'Visa Cash' is a competing product to MasterCard, Europay and Mondex. A Visa Cash trial was run at the 1996 Olympic Games in Atlanta. In response to this initiative, MasterCard took a 51 percent stake in Mondex in 1996 in an attempt to match Visa (Gandy, 1999, pp. 76–7; Srivastava and Mansell, 1998, p. 19). In 1997, Mondex developed a multi-application operating system – Multos[5] and marketed it as an open technology. Visa then launched the Open Platform multi-application system in 1998 to match Multos.

At the time that the major players (e.g. Visa, MasterCard/ Mondex) were carrying out trials in different countries, some European nations had already launched bank cards using smart card technology from 1994 onwards. However, the programs launched only featured domestic cards and were only used in closed or restricted environments (Bank for International Settlements, 2000). Table 5.2 lists the e-cash trial projects, both those conducted by domestic or regional financial institutions as well as by the major players, across Europe (European Central Bank, 2000).

In order to deliver smart cards for financial applications, EFTPOS terminals need to be equipped with smart card reader slots and ATMs need to be upgraded to be capable of accepting both existing magnetic stripe cards and smart cards. This requires capital expenditure of up to £1,300 per ATM terminal and up to £600 for an EFTPOS terminal to be upgraded to cope with smart card technology.

STANDARDS OF NETWORK INFRASTRUCTURE

With regard to the standard of network infrastructure for smart cards, the Global System for Mobile Communications (GSM) began its operations in 1992 for applications involving mobile services. GSM provides a standard for the smart card – the SIM card.[6] Another important standard for smart cards is EMV (Europay, MasterCard, Visa), equivalent to the magnetic stripe standard of 25 years ago and which was developed in 1993 as a standard for payment systems by MasterCard, Europay and Visa.

Table 5.2 Smart card e-cash applications in European countries

Country	Program	Commencing date	No. of cards ('000)		No. of loading machines	
			1997	1998	1997	1998
Belgium	Proton	1995	3,430	5,606	6,438	18,198
Denmark	Danmont	n/a	n/a	651	3	5
Germany	Geldkarte	1996	35,000	60,700	20,000	22,000
Spain	Visa Cash	1996	3,502	5,691	10,942	16,774
France	Modeus, Seme, Mondex	1996	n/a	n/a	n/a	n/a
Ireland	Visa Cash	n/a	—	3	—	20
Italy	Minipay	1994	62	56	945	916
Luxembourg	MiniCASH	n/a	—	—	—	—
Netherlands	Chipknip Chipper	1996	n/a	n/a	n/a	n/a
Austria	Quick	1994	3,400	3,700	3,495	4,954
Portugal	PMB	1995	384	411	5,129	5,834
Finland	Avant	n/a	189	324	2,100	2,208
Sweden	Cash	n/a	—	—	—	—
UK	Mondex, Visa Cash	1995	110	140	1,295	171
EU total			46,077	77,282	50,347	71,080

Source: Card Technology, October 1998, p. 54; Card Technology, Jan. 2000, p. 48; European Central Bank (2000, p. 201).

EMV is a specification for integrated circuit cards which fixes the dimensions and communications protocols of the cards so that all cards and card readers produced can work together (Gandy, 1999, p. 74; Kaplan, 1995, pp. 135, 184). Currently, the EMV chip is still dwarfed by the sheer number of magnetic stripe cards in circulation, although it is being accepted in a growing number of markets as countries migrate to chip cards.[7] Table 5.3 shows the milestones in smart card migration in different parts of the world.

Today, the smart card industry has not yet achieved inter-operability. There are competing smart card standards among the powerful players: Visa's Open Platform competes with Master-Card/Mondex's Multos, Proton World's Proton and Microsoft's Windows for Smart Cards, together with a plethora of in-house applications in the fields of transport, fixed line telephones and security, where inter-operability and global capability are

Table 5.3 Milestones in smart card migration

Area	Migration period	
	1999 Aug.	2001 Jan.
International, US, Canada	*Recommendations:* – All new devices should be chip and off-line PIN capable or upgradeable. – All new VISA ATMs to have chip and magnetic stripe readers.	All new Visa Smart Debit/ Smart Credit programs EMV/VIS compliant.
European Union	All new chip programs EMV/ VIS compliant.	
Central Europe, Middle East, Africa	All new Visa Smart Debit/ Smart Credit programs must be EMV/VIS compliant. *Recommendations:* – All new devices should be chip and offline PIN capable or upgradeable. – All new Visa ATMs should have chip and magnetic stripe reader.	All new chip card terminal devices (Visa Smart Debit/ Smart Credit programs) must also support off-line PIN functionality. All new Visa ATMs must have an EMV-compliant chip reader and magnetic stripe reader.

Source: Smart Path News (A Visa Smart Debit/Smart Credit publication), November 1999, pp. 4–5.

Table 5.3 (*continued*)

2002 Oct.	Oct.	2004 Jan.	2005 Jan.
		All new Visa Smart Debit/Smart Credit programs EMV/VIS compliant.	
– All chip programs EMV/VIS compliant. – New chip devices EMV compliant. – New chip devices PIN upgradeable. – New ATMs chip/ magnetic stripe capable. – Recertification of acquirer systems to support chip data.			Fraud liability shifts.
	– Acquiring systems must be capable of processing minimum chip data as defined by EMV. – Zero floor-limit magnetic stripe devices at high fraud loss merchants are to be replaced with EMV compliant devices. – All new terminals must be chip capable and EMV-compliant. – All existing chip terminals must be EMV compliant. – All existing (i.e. those started before August 1999) VSDC programs must be EMV/VIS compliant.		Fraud liability shifts.

Windows for Smart Cards is a smart-card operating system developed by Microsoft Corp. The system is designed to be used for corporate network access, Internet access and electronic cash and credit/debit transactions.

CEPS (Common Electronic Purse Specifications). This standard was created in 1999 to govern e-purse programs. The standard is planned for use in the application of e-cash. CEPS requires compatibility with the Europay, MasterCard, Visa (EMV) specifications for smart cards and defines the requirements for an inter-operable card application.

SET (Secure Electronic Transaction). The standard was launched in 1996 to tackle the problem of online card fraud. SET is an open technical standard developed by Visa and MasterCard. It relies on cryptography and digital certificates to ensure message confidentiality and security by authenticating cardholders and merchants. The SET standard provides a safe and reliable payment mechanism for shopping over the Internet.

unimportant. However, there is pressure for the smart card industry to have an inter-operable system for the e-cash application. This is because there is a current attempt to carry out chip migration towards the CEPS (Common Electronic Purse Specifications) standard. Since CEPS requires compatibility with the Europay, MasterCard, Visa (EMV) specifications, it is predicted among industry players that the new CEP standard will deliver inter-operability and create a multi-application environment. For e-commerce, SET (Secure Electronic Transaction) is established as a standard for secure payment over the Internet. The various challenges on standards have to be overcome before companies can compete on common capability products.[8]

MARKET COMPETITION

Currently, competitive contention in the smart card industry is feasible for many players. From the questionnaire survey, the

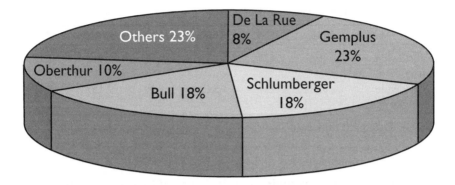

Figure 5.4 Worldwide smart card vendors – unit shipment market share (1998)
Source: Gartner Group, 2000.

Table 5.4 Smart card market forecast

Market Segment	1997 (millions of units)	2003 (millions of units)	Compound Annual Growth Rate (%)
Public Telephone	684	3,270	30
Wireless	69	760	49
Banking	49	690	55
Loyalty	22	320	56
Health	16	210	54
Pay TV	12	150	52
Transport	8	240	77
Gaming	2	70	78
Access Control	10	260	72
Identity	2	50	71
Information Technology	1	120	142
Other	24	170	38
Total	900	6,310	38

Source: Visa International, 2000.

industry players see that the future of smart cards is going to be a combination of financial and non-financial applications. Therefore, there are many combinations of financial and non-financial innovators who are seeking to exploit the smart card

Table 5.5 Worldwide chip card forecast

Units (million)	1998	1999	2000	2001	2002	2003
Worldwide smart card	296	439	551	720	914	1,238
Worldwide memory card	958	1,257	1,545	1,841	2,157	2,496

Source: Dataquest European Semiconductor Group, Gartner Group, 2000.

technology as part of their overall financial business strategy.

The competitors in the mobile telephony market have already released Wireless Application Protocol (WAP) phones; Nokia, Motorola, Sony, and Ericsson, the major mobile phone players, all offer smart phones with WAP Internet services. Nokia is now pursuing the 'Global IP Mobility strategy' to extend its mobile functionality to offer mobile banking jointly with Visa.[9] Industry analysts predict that m-commerce, a convergence of card payments and mobile telephony, will be poised for exponential

WAP (Wireless Application Protocol)
WAP technology is used in the SIM (Subscriber Identity Module) card, offering value-added services such as mobile banking and Internet access. The smart SIM card provides mobile users with access to the digital cellular system. The smart SIM card is personalised to a specific mobile phone user to provide phone compatibility. Nokia was the first company to launch WAP phones in 1999. The major competitors in the WAP-enabled phone market are Nokia, Motorola, Sony and Ericsson.

Global IP Mobility strategy
Nokia competes to take advantage of the liberalisation of the telecoms market by focussing on the home communications sector. Nokia uses the Global IP (Internet Protocol) Mobility strategy to build a strong position in mobile telephony. Given that the home is increasingly integrated with the office and other personal environments, Nokia aims to use its strength in digital technologies (broadband technology, fast Internet access solutions, wireless local networks) to build a broad customer base in the home communications market.

> **m-commerce** is the use of mobile phones to provide payment services. M-commerce reflects a change in distribution technology innovations in the card payment industry. Mobile banking functions as a phone channel, meaning banks no longer have to depend on the branch network in order to reach the customer frontier. As competition increases, banks realise the importance of providing integrated delivery channels: branch, phone, Internet, digital television and hand-held computers all add value to the traditional card-based services.

growth over the next few years. The development of a smart card for mobile phone application is shown in figure 5.5. Table 5.6 shows that Nokia, Motorola and Ericsson, who were the early movers in the mobile phone market, held their positions as the leading mobile manufacturers in the cellular system business in the late 1990s. Since the European market is the most advanced in terms of mobile phones, penetration of European households gives a reasonable picture of the growth in the mobile phone market (table 5.7).

LOYALTY CARDS

In the loyalty card market, although the majority of loyalty schemes are still based on magnetic stripe technology, many companies are racing to exploit the full potential of smart loyalty

Table 5.6 Worldwide mobile phones market share 1999 (in millions of units)

Rank	Company	Sales	Market share (%)
1	Nokia	76.3	26.9
2	Motorola	47.8	16.9
3	Ericsson	29.8	10.5
4	Samsung	17.7	6.2
5	Panasonic	15.6	5.5
	Others	96.4	34.0
	Total	283.6	100.0

Source: Nokia Corp., Vertical Facts, Figures and Forecasts, May 2001, p. 17.

Innovation Process

1970

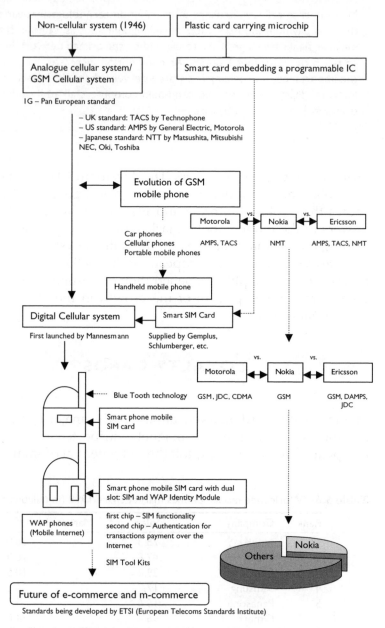

Figure 5.5 The development of smart cards for mobile phone applications
Source: The author's design.

Table 5.7 Penetration of interactive technologies (in percentages of homes)

UK	1997	1998	1999[1]	2000[1]	2001[1]	2002[1]	2003[1]
Internet	8	14	17	29	—	—	—
Interactive Digital TV	—	—	3	13	21	29	34
GSM Mobile Phones	15	23	33	41	48	—	—

Europe	1997	1998	1999[1]	2000[1]	2001[1]	2002[1]	2003[1]
Internet	7.6	11.9	16.5	23	24.8	29.3	—
Interactive Digital TV	—	—	2	4	7	9	12
GSM Mobile Phones	—	—	—	4.4	6.9	9.8	12.7

Source: Morgan Stanley Dean Witter, European Internet Report, June 1999.

[1] Estimated figures

cards. Shell Oil UK was the first to launch a large-scale programme of loyalty cards in 1994. Shell invested £20 million in its Shell Smart[10] programme with a plan to generate return visits to its petrol stations by encouraging motorists to collect loyalty points.[11] To date, Shell has attracted 5 million members to its Shell Smart programme. Although the Shell Smart card cannot presently be used as a payment card, Shell has identified the integration of its loyalty and payment products into one card as a key part of its future plans.[12] Boots took the innovative lead in the retail business by launching the Boots Advantage Loyalty Card in 1999. By co-branding with Egg, the on-line bank, Boots is hoping to establish its position against WalMart with a card that not only offers flexible loyalty programmes but also combines loyalty and credit card functionality.[13]

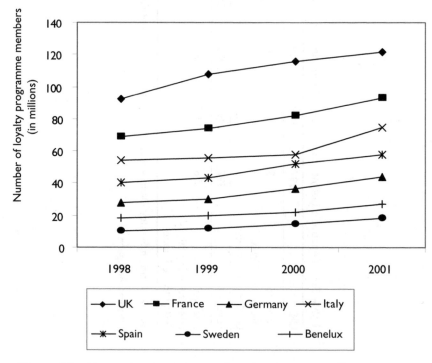

Figure 5.6 The market development of loyalty programmes: Europe
Source: Datamonitor.

In airline loyalty schemes, American Express (Amex) is regarded as the leader of the global programmes with its Membership Rewards scheme. Amex pursued the strategy to use

Innovation process

1970

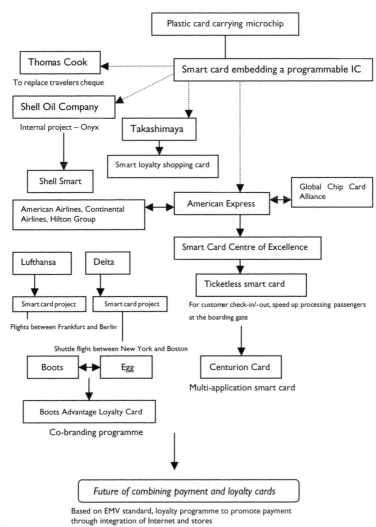

2002

Figure 5.7 The development of smart loyalty cards

Source: The author's design.

its brand strength to provide the customers with special recognition by focussing on frequent flyers (Kaplan, 1995, pp. 258–9; Shaw, 1991). Amex set up the Smart Card Centre of Excellence in 1995 as its first step towards a comprehensive multi-application travel and entertainment product. The company carried out technological research into the concept of using smart card technologies to deliver ticketless airline travel – the ultimate travel card scheme.[14] Seeing the future of smart cards in loyalty programmes as the integration of Internet access and payment, Amex launched the Blue Card in 1999 with the on-line strategy to capture customers making purchases over the Internet.[15]

Figure 5.6 shows the market development in smart card loyalty applications in European countries. It can be seen that the UK is pioneering the loyalty card programme.

In the late 1990s, smart card contactless technology has also been adopted by transport operators. Since the typical transit payment is of low value but high volume, the contactless smart card is appropriate for use across the transport network. With a contactless smart card, passengers merely walk near the terminal. Sensors read the information stored in the chip as the passengers board trains and buses (The Smart Card Forum, 1997, p. 181). The Creative Star in Hong Kong launched the first smart card system – the Octopus smart card fare payment system – in 1997. The payment system cost £30 million and covers all modes of public transport.[16] The transit operators hope to earn a share of the float, or interest, on the cash collected on these pre-payment cards since there is always a delay before the credits are used and a percentage of the stored value on cards is never used. They also see opportunities to consolidate their transport smart card with

Contactless technology

Contactless technology is generally used for physical access control applications. Applications such as electronic payment, electronic ticketing and transit can be combined with physical access to offer a multi-application and multi-technology ID credential. Contactless smart cards authenticate a cardholder's identity, determine the appropriate level of access and admit the cardholder to a facility, all from data stored on the card. Contactless smart cards offer organizations the flexibility to select appropriate technologies driven by business requirements.

Table 5.8 Leading transit smart card fare systems worldwide

Region	Programmes	
North America	Montreal	Los Angeles
	Toronto	Ann Arbor
	Washington, D.C.	Atlanta
South America	São Paulo	Mexico City
	Buenos Aires	
Europe	London	Paris
	Oslo	Marseilles
	Manchester	Barcelona
	Liverpool	Berlin
	Helsinki	Östersund, Uppsala, & Luelå
	Amsterdam	København
Asia	Tokyo	Sydney
	Hong Kong	Melbourne
	Singapore	

Source: SCF Working Group on Transportation cited in The Smart Card Forum (1997, p. 182).

e-cash applications. This is because the number of transport users and transaction volumes of the transport system are large. Also, the syndicate nature of public transport gives the transport companies an almost unbreakable customer hold. This provides them with the opportunity, together with a junior partner, to add payment functionality to their transport cards. Table 5.8 shows the worldwide application of smart cards for fare payment in the late 1990s.

Contactless cards are increasingly accepted as the credential of choice for controlling physical access.

Recognising a similar opportunity in the Internet business, the telephone operators GTE Corp. and Bell Canada changed their strategy not only to the issuing of smart telephone cards but also serving as providers of web security and electronic data transmission networks.[17] Competition in the smart telephone card market increased as the phone card issuers teamed up with bank card issuers and merchants. For example, US West, the US telephone company, teamed up with American Express in 1998 to allow the smart telephone card to function as a payment card. Similarly, AT&T tailored its existing Internet services to focus on

SMART CARDS

Innovation process

1970

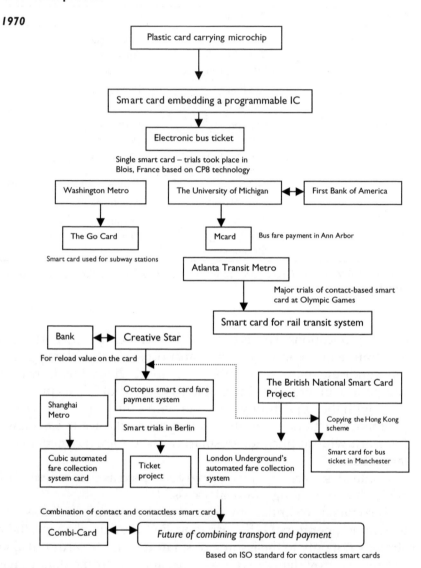

Figure 5.8 The development of smart cards for transport
Source: The author's design.

Innovation process

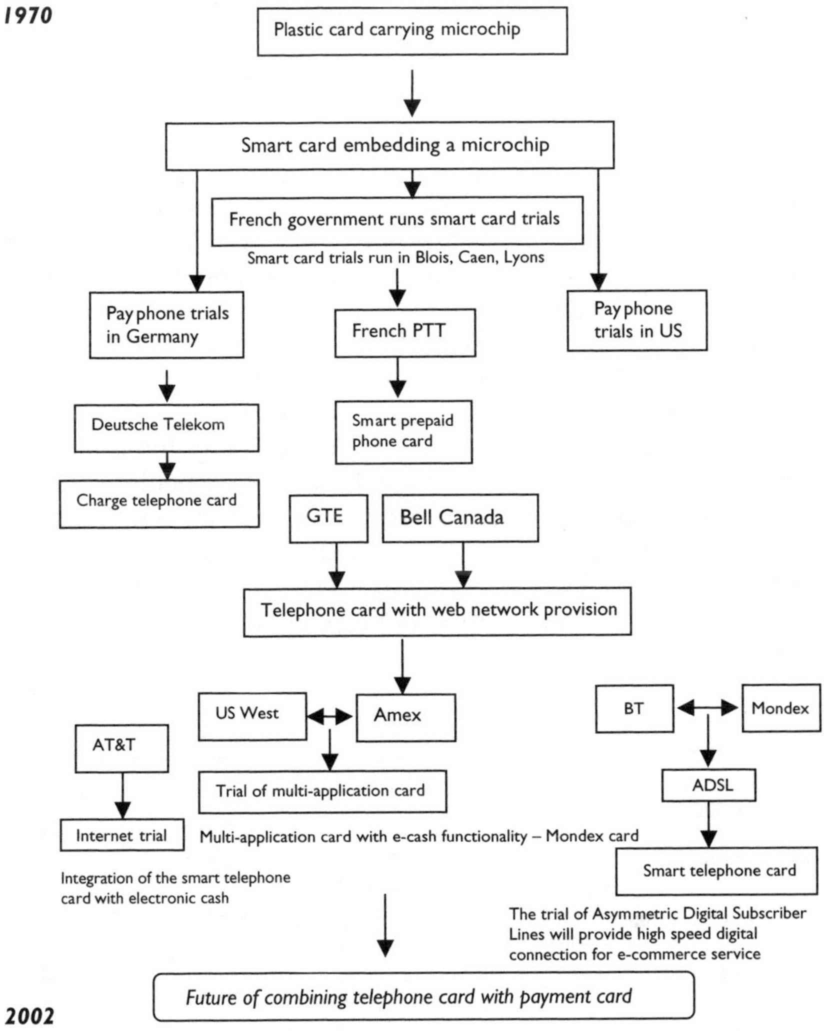

1970

```
            ┌─────────────────────────────────┐
            │  Plastic card carrying microchip │
            └─────────────────────────────────┘
                            │
            ┌─────────────────────────────────┐
            │  Smart card embedding a microchip│
            └─────────────────────────────────┘
                            │
            ┌───────────────────────────────────────┐
            │ French government runs smart card trials│
            └───────────────────────────────────────┘
            Smart card trials run in Blois, Caen, Lyons
```

| Pay phone trials in Germany | French PTT | Pay phone trials in US |

Deutsche Telekom

Smart prepaid phone card

Charge telephone card

GTE   Bell Canada

Telephone card with web network provision

US West ←→ Amex

AT&T

Trial of multi-application card

BT ←→ Mondex

ADSL

Internet trial   Multi-application card with e-cash functionality – Mondex card

Smart telephone card

Integration of the smart telephone card with electronic cash

The trial of Asymmetric Digital Subscriber Lines will provide high speed digital connection for e-commerce service

Future of combining telephone card with payment card

2002

Figure 5.9   The development of smart telephone cards
Source: The author's design.

Table 5.9 European interactive digital TV customers, 1999–2004

	1999	2000	2001	2002	2003	2004
Customers ('000s)	69	573	1,525	3,065	4,700	6,121

Source: Datamonitor.

the e-cash market by integrating its smart telephone card with electronic cash functionality.[18] In 1997, AT&T launched an Internet trial to enable cardholders to upload and download cash from banks and purchase small dollar items on the World Wide Web.[19] BT also worked with Mondex UK in 1999 to combine payphone functionality and e-commerce services.

The smart card-based payment system for pay TV service represents another opportunity in converging Internet technology with digital TV technology. In the theory behind pay TV, a customer could buy a smart card loaded with currency, against which viewing hours would be deducted via a set-top box decoder. The pay TV service operator Telenor Conax was the first to expand pay TV services by enabling customers to pay by e-cash in 1998.[20]

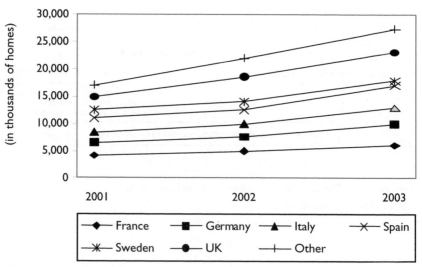

Figure 5.10 European set-top box smart card reader installed base
Source: Datamonitor.

Table 5.9 shows the growth in the smart card-based payment system for digital TV in Europe according to a Datamonitor report.

It can be seen that the competition in smart cards and their use in various financial applications will be intensifying as contenders encompass not only the traditional banks but other industry players. Figures 5.11, 5.12 and table 5.10 show the

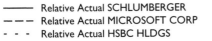

———— Relative Actual SCHLUMBERGER
— — — Relative Actual MICROSOFT CORP
- - - Relative Actual HSBC HLDGS
- - - - Relative Actual SHELL REFINING(FOM)
———— Relative Actual NOKIA CORP
- - - - - - Relative Actual ERICSSON TELECOMMUICACOES SA
— — — Relative Actual AMERICAN EXPRESS CO
- - - - - Relative Actual BOOTS CO

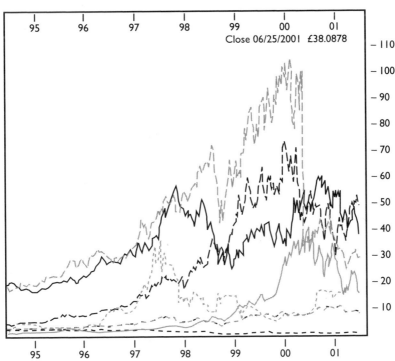

Figure 5.11 The share price of major players attempting to offer smart cards for financial applications
Source: Hydra.

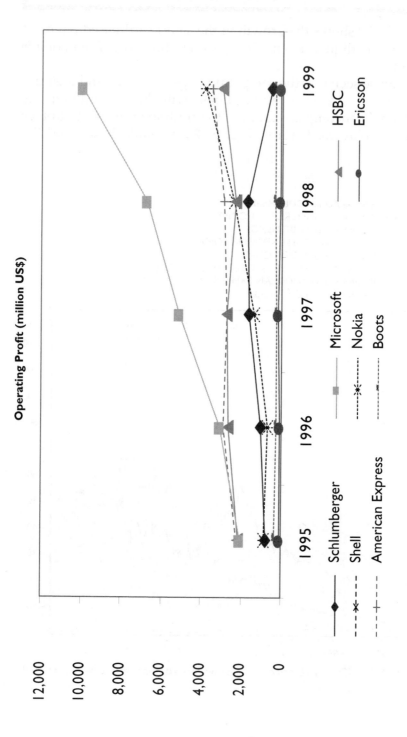

Operating Profit (million US$)

Schlumberger	Microsoft	HSBC
Shell	Nokia	Ericsson
American Express	Boots	

Figure 5.12 Operating profit and market-to-book value of major players attempting to offer smart cards for financial applications
Source: Datastream.

Market-to-Book Value

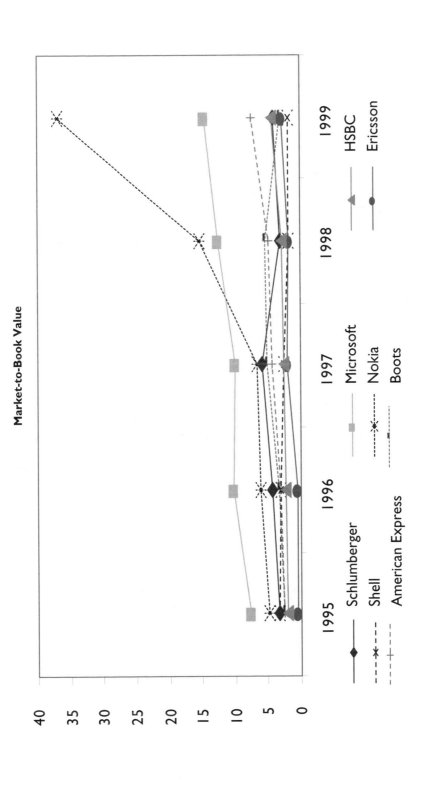

Schlumberger Microsoft HSBC
Shell Nokia Ericsson
American Express Boots

Table 5.10 Market value of major players attempting to offer smart cards for financial applications (in millions of US dollars)

Market value	1995	1996	1997	1998	1999
Schlumberger	16,750	24,598	40,067	25,316	30,860
Microsoft	51,975	98,752	155,965	345,826	602,432
HSBC	5,419	7,288	8,060	8,673	46,294
Shell	9,149	9,211	7,593	4,979	5,377
Nokia	5,834	9,103	13,652	47,211	200,631
Ericsson	258	267	995	878	1,414
American Express	20,042	26,774	41,482	46,339	74,426
Boots	3,497	3,499	4,726	5,638	3,451

Source: Datastream.

overall financial performance of the players attempting to offer smart cards for financial applications. Overall, Microsoft performs better than the other contenders and has the most resources and capabilities. Although the share price of Microsoft is falling, the market-to-book value and market value still suggest that Microsoft has a good return potential. Nokia, despite the slump in the telecom sector, still has a competitive position as the leader in GSM mobile telephony. American Express has a large market capitalisation and a competitive position in the travel and entertainment industries. Since Amex is also a bank and a major issuer of pre-paid financial credits in the form of travellers cheques, it has the capability and sufficient business cover across the markets to make electronic payments a reality. Amex's continued research in smart card technology also suggests its intended challenge in offering the smart card charge card.

FUTURE OF THE SMART CARD INNOVATION

The state of development in which some significant players have now recognised the importance of the smart card technology and its multi-function purposes illustrate the need for collaboration across the industries. The application of smart card e-cash is, so far, less developed because it is expensive to change the financial infrastructure in the physical world. There is controversy over cost-benefit sharing across the infrastructure, which requires cooperation from the retailers; the retailers see no benefit from this deal. From their point of view, if they have to accept the card (where the benefits seem to be limited to banks), then retailers will do that only when banks agree to pay for the terminal installation costs. Visa International expressed concerns about the high cost of investment (particularly for the multi-function smart card). The senior officer of Visa International stated:

"Yes, the costs are significant. For Europe as a whole, we estimate a total figure of eight billion dollars. Two-and-a-half billion on the cards. Four billion on the systems. And the remaining one-and-a-half billion on the terminals and ATMs. And yes, eight billion is a lot of money. But it's not correct to think about it as an isolated, ring-fenced figure. Because, when you consider the on-going costs of maintaining the current mag-stripe infrastructure, then I'd suggest that – over a five year time-scale – this eight billion represents an incremental investment of no more than five percent. And what could that five percent buy you ? Of course fraud reduction, of course multi-application. But we have a yet more compelling reason – the reality of the Internet" (Hans van der Velde, President, Visa International EU Region)

There is still an ongoing development of different standards among smart cards. Although there are attempts to carry out trials for each standard in different countries, these trials are going nowhere. Many pilots in Europe's national trials were cancelled. The two major smart card trials in New York and Guelph, Canada were called off. Other trials, such as those that have taken place in Britain, Canada and New Zealand have all been met with apathy. Customers still prefer cash and view the way innovators are trying to change their behaviour as

Market Pull
The linear model of R&D with a simple one-way flow of ideas from market/consumer to innovation development. Innovation involves the recognition of a need or a potential market for a new product or process. The 'market pull' or 'demand pull' theory of innovation is characterised by a strong market demand that theoretically leads to the necessary inventions and innovations.

'Technology Push' rather than 'Market Pull'. Mondex International expressed concerns over future multi-function applications, stating that although the multi-function smart card will remove the need to carry a multitude of cards, there are still two major problems: *who is to use it* and *how*. Even though today the functionality of four or five applications is available on a smart card, it is still very expensive, and thus would create a limited opportunity to get a significant return and achieve the level of cost-effectiveness the innovator would expect.

The smart card industry reflects a situation where competition for players developing smart cards for financial applications is intense. It will be hard for innovators in the traditional banking sector to compete for competitive advantage. This is because innovations in smart cards for financial applications potentially arise outside as well as within the banking sector. To put it another way, smart cards for financial applications need not necessarily be issued by financial institutions since electronic payments can be made without requiring a network for clearing and settlements. Such a network does not give banks a clear advantage in launching successful smart cards for financial applications.

The competition in innovating smart cards for financial applications can be considered against three scenarios. These scenarios are not predictions for the future, but show possible paths to three plausible development outcomes for the smart card industry. In each scenario, the outer circle represents the revenue pool of innovation. The inner circle represents the market share of the individual innovators (smart card issuers).

(1) The first scenario

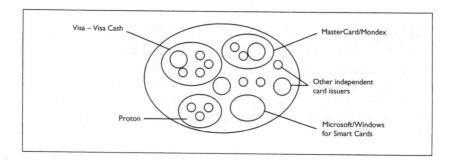

The first scenario represents a continuation of the current situation. That is, the competition among the major groups of innovators results in the development of different standards: Visa – the Open Platform; MasterCard/Mondex – Multos; Proton World – Proton. Competitors outside the banking industry in mobile telephony, retail business and the airline industry continue to the point where they deliver smart cards for financial applications to their customer base.

(2) The second scenario

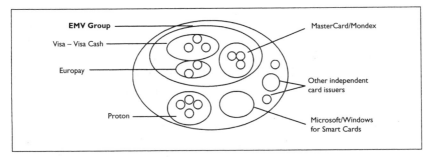

The second scenario reflects successful collaboration among innovators competing to launch smart cards. In other words, this scenario represents the situation where the players of Europay, MasterCard and Visa, in forming an EMV group, are successful in imposing an EMV standard. Innovators can optimise the EMV standard to provide the service on an extended basis to an enlarged market. By forming larger networks, innovators can hope to enjoy the benefits in terms of extended locations for card use without having further investment in terminals for the delivery of smart card-based services.

(3) The third scenario
The third scenario represents the possibility of a single innovator dominating the smart card industry. Microsoft is seen as the most likely innovator to have this potential. Currently, Microsoft uses a competitive strategy to promote Windows for Smart Cards. Its strong position in the Personal Computer (PC) operating system market gives Microsoft the opportunity to exploit the strength of its position provided by ownership of over 90% of PC customers. Microsoft owns the technology for Windows for

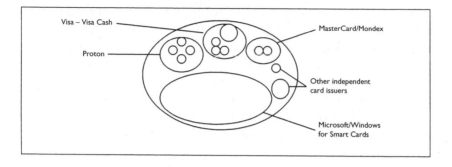

Smart Cards and has the financial resources to overcome the difficulties of high capital investment (cost of upgrading ATMs and EFTPOS to accept smart cards). Thus, Microsoft prefers to go it alone. Microsoft is confident that the internal benefits would be attractive even if collaboration with other innovators remains a possibility.

The smart card market depicts a situation where organisations compete to launch different technologies: Visa's Open Platform, MasterCard/Mondex's Multos, Proton World's Proton and Microsoft's Windows for Smart Cards. Innovators (smart card issuers) see the benefits of standard competition in terms of a network externality effect. If innovators could impose their standard as de facto in the market, the established standard could help their cards to achieve a wide level of diffusion. In other words, the competitive position of the companies can be significantly affected by their ability to establish a technology as an industry standard. However, many industry players agree that it

Open Platform is a card management specification that allows rapid development of globally inter-operable smart card systems. It enables smart card terminals or readers from multiple manufacturers to access information on open-platform encoded cards. Visa Open Platform uses JavaCard to support its competitive programme for the inter-operability of smart cards. The founding members of Visa Open Platform represent a cross-industry demographic, including telecommunications, banking, technology and government (e.g. BT, Carte Bleue, Gemplus, Hitachi, JCB, Keycorp and NEC).

Multos

Multos (Multi-purpose Operating System) is a platform that supports multi-application functionality. Multos was developed by a consortium – MAOSCO. This consortium, composed of three semiconductor companies – Hitachi, Motorola and Siemens – and five smart card companies – Mondex International, MasterCard, Gemplus, Dai Nippon Printing and Keycorp – has been formed to support the Multi-Application Operating System, a specification that includes an operating system and development platform for secure smart cards. The new operating system allows interaction between functionalities of applications for use in a wide area of applications, e.g. the function of payment, loyalty, transit and GSM SIM card on a single card.

will be hard to achieve wide diffusion and accessibility if they cannot agree on cross-platform standards. They emphasise the importance of multi-party interdependence. Visa, the owner of Open Platform technology, stated that 'there's no point fighting for technology. The most important is the business and the applications . . . ' Multos, its main rival in terms of technology claimed that 'there's nothing wrong with competing for different areas of the market so long as it has a role on the same base . . . ' Their statements represent an effort to establish the same technology-based development before beginning to compete in the marketplace.

The major players in the smart card business claim that the marketing of smart cards will depend on the extent to which the issuer can offer customised services. They predict that aggressive competing activity is likely because the card functionalities will, more or less, be embedded within one card. Thus, the ground of competition seems not to be based on the indi-

Proton World's Proton

Proton World develops Proton technology for use in smart card payment applications and electronic purse systems. The Proton-based smart card was developed to give a boost to common smart card and electronic purse standards. In Belgium, the Proton card is aiming to set a precedent by being the first electronic purse scheme in the country.

vidual card functionality but a package of card functionalities.

Now more than 27 years on since its first inception, the smart card industry has progressed very slowly. It has not yet achieved inter-operability. There are also competing smart card standards which means that any process of innovation is effectively prevented from achieving a level of wide adoption. Industry opinion provides reasonable insights into near-term smart card innovation and the diversity of industry views at this relatively late stage in the technical evolution of smart cards is itself inter-esting. However, whether smart cards will achieve wide, even global, usage or not can only be empirically observable in the long term.

> "Everything will be different from what we expect. Of course, no one knows for sure what the future may bring. But, by moving ahead, by investing in the payment system, by upgrading the payment infra-structure, by appreciating and grasping the promise, new business opportunities are there for the taking." (Hans van der Velde, President Visa International EU Region)

SUMMARY

In a fast-moving and competitive industry, there are many oppor-tunities for all competitors to develop smart cards for financial applications. This chapter built upon the empirical findings in previous chapters to understand the protracted innovation process and continued uncertainty in the dominant mode of diffusion for smart cards. A central issue is the way in which the players in the smart card industry see their options in exploiting collaborative solutions as a means to achieve diffusion.

Innovation diffusion requires network externality to complete the interactions of card applications. In other words, smart cards need an extensive network across various industries e.g. banking, retailing, credit card organisations and telecommunications for successful implementation. ARM Limited said, 'Technology is not a problem. The problem is having the agreement between the different network providers, software providers and so on. It is the content, the applications that will take more time to develop. And it's the chicken and egg situation. Nobody will develop the applications if the card is not there . . . '[21]

Standards for inter-operability are important for smart cards to achieve a level of diffusion. However, the development of smart cards was undertaken under competing standards by Visa's Open Platform, MasterCard/Mondex's Multos and Microsoft's Smart Card for Windows. The difficulty seems to be that the leading card associations envisage that agreement on one standard system will create a significant disadvantage to them in the sense of loss of control (all the potential advantages of imposing their own standard are lost) and thus they tend to compete to get their standards accepted in the consumer market. Also, innovators regard that standard as a domain to recover their R&D costs and therefore having one standard means losing some investment. Seemingly, while innovators are seen to co-operate on standards and the negotiations of such agreement have been carried out, in practice smart card development is still actioned on a competitive basis.

Although the smart card is going to provide more value in terms of multi-applications, there are difficulties in understanding the market requirement. The interviews conducted reveal that it is probably too early to conclude that customers really need one banking card which has the payment functions to interact with other applications. Another concern is that there is feedback from the customers that a single card is not a viable proposition since they do not want their health data to be put together with loyalty programmes. Concerning price, even though today the functionality of several applications is available on the smart card, it is still very expensive, and thus would possibly create a limited opportunity to get the return and achieve cost-effectiveness that the innovator would expect.

Concerning the ongoing development of smart cards, many interviewees emphasised that the marketing activities will depend on the extent to which the issuer can offer customised services. They viewed that aggressive competing activity is likely because all the card functionalities will, more or less, be embedded within one card. Thus, the ground of competition seems not to be based on the individual card functionality but a package of card functionalities where establishing a brand is seen as the main thrust of marketing. Be that as it may, the player that can persuade the customers to use the card may be critical to a continuing advantage, in the sense that a whole series of customised applications may drive the introduction to critical masses as well as increase retention and loyalty in its own right through reinforcing desired behaviour with issuer and multi-merchant schemes.

Currently, there are major competitors (Visa, MasterCard/ Mondex, Proton World and Microsoft) competing to launch smart cards in a multi-application environment. Until these major parties realise that competition will hold back the process of innovation diffusion, collaboration will not take place. Some bankers suggest that in order to be successful, there needs to be a certain party[22] to lobby the process at a regulatory and legislative level in order to make smart card diffusion happen more quickly. Some firms in the area of information technology also suggest that the smart card, to be successful, needs to be led by government legislation so that all players can follow the same path.

From the study, the state of development in which some significant players have now recognised the importance of smart card roll out illustrates the need of collaboration across industries. However, there are still many obstacles to overcome in order to move to multi-applications. So what can be done, wait and do nothing or completely re-engineer? Arguably, some industry players suggest that it is too late to change now but continue ahead on the same path because too much time and money has been invested. With respect to this, it might be relevant that the issues about market acceptance, the standards for interoperability and cost-benefit sharing have to be accompanied by a sacrifice of some degree of competition (as suggested by the case of ATM/cash cards, credit cards and EFTPOS/debit cards in previous chapters).

Notes

Chapter 1   *ATM/Cash Cards*

1   History of Cash Dispensers – Barclays Group Archives.
2   *Banking World*, July 1986, p. 28.
3   This was because the bank at that time concentrated on the wholesale deposit market rather than the retail deposit market. The current account balance of Barclays slightly increased from £2,362 million in 1969 to £2,448 million in 1970 (4% increase) (*Barclays Bulletin*, 1967–1968; Company Annual Reports).
4   *Barclays Business Development Personal Sector*, July 1978, p. 3; *Barclaynews*, October 1985, p. 1; *Barclaynews*, March 1986, pp. 8–9.
5   *Computers in Banking*, February 1988, p. 18.
6   Financial Statistics, December 1989.
7   *Banking Technology Supplement – Building Societies*, October 1989, p. 12.
8   *Banking World*, November 1988, p. 15; November 1989, p. 38.
9   The reciprocity was in terms of paying the annual membership fee of around £10,000 (*Banking World*, October 1988, p. 19).
10 LINK Interchange Network, Ltd.
11 Barclays did at first consider investment in ATMs not for the purpose of competing for market share, but for cost reduction purpose.
12 According to the study by LINK Interchange Network, banks with large networks did not gain from acquiring more transactions. By definition, in a closed system, the net issued and acquired charges amount to zero. Although in practice it is likely that larger banks may exploit their competitive position (from owning more ATMs) in terms of demanding higher fees for access to their own systems, there are also other factors like siting, branding, card issuing and charging strategies (Cruickshank, 2000, p. 284; LINK Interchange Network).

Chapter 2   *Credit Cards*

1   An interchange fee is a payment made by the merchant acquirer to the card issuer to cover the cost of services provided by card issuers to retailers and merchant acquirers (Cruickshank, 2000, p. 255).
2   The merchant service charge is the charge made to merchants by merchant-acquiring banks on the value of transactions made by payment cards (Lindsey, 1994, p. 126). The percentage of charges vary

between 1.6 and 4 percent of the value of each transaction (Worthington, 1996, p. 66).

3 *Barclays Bulletin*, No. 39, Summer 1975, p. 3.
4 From Barclaycard's viewpoint, it envisaged that there were complexities involved in adopting a US system for UK use, including: integration with feeder systems for capturing voucher details, customer payments (as the US had a radically different banking system), authorisations (which was then an intense manual process), Country Club Billing (where individual transaction slips were matched and sent out with the statement) and address formats/postcodes which were very different from the United States model (from interviews with Barclaycard).
5 *Banking World*, October 1988, p. 19.
6 Barclaycard Media Information.
7 Barclaycard Media Information.
8 Key Note Market Report – Credit and Other Finance Cards, 1999, p. 50.
9 The nature of the contract is short-term which provides a condition to be renewed every 2–3 years. The mobile phone company will pay commission to banks according to the proportion of customers making calls via mobile phones (from interviews with BT Cellnet).
10 It was advised that the brand strength of Barclaycard was also from its marketing strategy to introduce the card under its own brand. From the issuing point of view, the conglomeration of banks under the name Access was considered as lacking identity of the individual bank presence in terms of market competition (from interviews with Barclaycard).
11 Barclaycard Media Information.
12 Barclaycard's competitive advantage can also be explained by its highest charge of annual percentage rate (APR rate). Although Barclaycard reduced the APR rate from 27% in the 1970s–80s to around 19% in the late 1990s, the lowering interest rate does not represent an accurate interest rate reduction. This is because the bank base rate during the same period also fell, from 12% to around 6%. The differential shows that Barclaycard still earns the same level of percentage points (*Bank of England Quarterly Bulletin*).

Chapter 3   *EFTPOS/Debit Cards*

1 Data Encryption Standard – encryption algorithm.
2 *Banking World*, September 1988, p. 60.
3 *The Banker*, April 1984, p. 91; *Banking Technology*, April 1986, p. 16.
4 *Banking Technology*, May 1989, p. 16; *The Banker*, September 1988, p. 92.
5 *Banking World*, September 1988, pp. 60–3.
6 Smith and Wield, 1988, p. 268; data obtained from LINK Interchange Network Ltd.
7 The Unified Debit Card Scheme, or UDCS, of EFTPOS UK was a network operation and commercial arrangement consisting of a set of

technical standards. Banks would issue debit cards and all EFTPOS UK terminals would accept these cards under the UDCS agreement (Howells and Hine, 1993, p. 73).

8   LINK Interchange Network Ltd.
9   *Banking Technology*, July/August 1987, p. 14.
10 *Banking Technology*, September 1991, p. 56.
11 Maestro International was created as an equal partnership joint venture between Europay International and MasterCard International. The Maestro brand was introduced as the world's first truly global one hundred percent on-line EPOS debit service (*Key Note – Credit & Other Finance Cards*, 1999, p. 29).
12 *American Banker*, 16 November 1993, Vol. 158(219), p. 14.
13 The ability to issue cards does not drive the number of current accounts. Rather, the number of debit cards on issue is dependent on the total number of current accounts.

Chapter 4   *Competition, Innovation and Performance: The Evolution of the Bank Card Business*

1   *APACS Plastic Card Review*, 1999; *APACS Yearbook of Payment Statistics*, 1999.
2   When the nature of the innovation has strong customer hold, the marketing of the innovation can be based on the existing customer base. The selling of the innovation does not depend on the characteristics of innovation (product differentiation). For example, ATM/cash cards have no difficulties in respect of product differentiation. The marketing of the card innovation is tied to the current account customers (having strong customer hold).
    When the nature of the innovation has low customer hold, the marketing of the innovation can rarely be based on the existing customer base. The selling of the innovation is often determined by the characteristics of innovation (product differentiation). For example, Consumer electronic products have difficulties in marketing with product differentiation. There are difficulties in selling the product to the existing customers because of the low customer hold.

Chapter 5   *Smart Cards*

1   The rate of substitution is discussed in Fisher and Pry (1971). However, smart card technology seems not to be a competitive substitution for the magnetic stripe card. Since both technologies have co-existed for some time (from the inception of the smart card), this suggests that smart card technology may not substitute at all. Therefore, it is difficult to forecast the rate of substitution of smart cards for magnetic stripe cards at present.
2   According to the concept of technology substitution by Fisher and Pry, smart cards may not be a competitive substitution for magnetic stripe

cards since the underlying technologies have co-existed for a long time (from the inception of the smart card).

3   *Mondex Magazine,* July 1997, pp. 29–30.

4   However, these two major trials were later called off. Also, the other trials, such as those that took place in Britain, Canada and New Zealand, have all been met with apathy (*The Economist,* 21 November 1998, p. 73). The failure of e-purse implementation has now raised the question of whether it is time for banks to abandon the e-purse market (Payment Systems Europe Limited, Smart Card conference, 2000).

5   The operating system Multos was developed by a consortium – MAOSCO. This consortium, composed of three semiconductor companies – Hitachi, Motorola and Siemens – and five smart card companies – Mondex International, MasterCard, Gemplus, Dai Nippon Printing and Keycorp – has been formed to support Multi-Application Operation System, a specification that includes an operating system and development platform for secure smart cards (*Electronic Business Today,* Vol. 23(7), July 1997, p. 24). A new operating system allows for interaction between the functionalities of applications for use in a wide variety of applications, e.g. the function of payment, loyalty, transit and GSM SIM card on a single card.

6   GSM-enabled phones are equipped with SIM (Subscriber Identity Module) cards. The phones may be incompatible, but the cards are not and this allows the users to use the cards in any GSM phone (*World Trade,* Vol. 11(7), July 1998, pp. 70–2).

7   *Chip Directions,* A Visa Smart Publication, October 1999.

8   Card Forum International, September/October 1998, p. 59.

9   *The Banker,* February 2001, Vol. 151(900), p. 88; Nokia Corp. – Facts, Figures and Forecasts, May 2001, p. 39.

10 *Marketing,* 6 October 1994, p. 13.

11 *Credit Card Management,* Vol. 10(10), January 1998, pp. 16–18.

12 *Marketing,* 29 March 2001, p. 1.

13 *Loyalty,* August 1998, p. 12.

14 Smart Card Initiatives, Travel and Entertainment, American Express.

15 American Express Company Annual Report 1999, p. 14; *Credit Card Management,* Vol. 12(1), April 1999, pp. 132–6.

16 *International Railway Journal,* February 2000, p. 35; *The Intelligent Highway,* 31 January 2000, p. 8; *Urban Transport International,* January/February 2000, p. 24.

17 *Card Technology,* October 1998, p. 8.

18 *Bank Marketing,* February 1998, Vol. 30(2), pp. 40–6.

19 *Mondex Magazine,* July 1997, p. 25.

20 *Mondex Magazine,* March 1999, p. 22.

21 Mr. Jean De Oliveira – European Segment Sales Manager, ARM Ltd.

22 It was mentioned that this party is likely to be the retailers since they have a strong position in the market place.

References

Annual Abstract of Banking Statistics (1993), Statistical Unit, British Bankers Association, London.

APACS (1995), Yearbook of Payment Statistics 1995, London: Association for Payment Clearing Services.

APACS (1996), Yearbook of Payment Statistics 1996, London: Association for Payment Clearing Services.

APACS (1999), Yearbook of Payment Statistics 1999, London: Association for Payment Clearing Services.

APACS (1999), Plastic Card Review 1999, London: Association for Payment Clearing Services.

Bank for International Settlements (2000), *Survey of Electronic Money Developments*, Committee on Payment and Settlement Systems Secretariat, Basel, Switzerland.

Bright, R. (1988), *Smart Cards: Principles, Practice, Applications*, Chichester: John Wiley & Sons.

Brown, S. and R. Brown (1987), *The Smart Card*, Somerset: POST-NEWS.

Chorafas, D. N. (1988), *Electronic Funds Transfer*, London: Butterworths.

Cruickshank, D. (2000), *Competition in UK Banking – Report to the Chancellor of the Exchequer* (http://www.bankreview.org.uk).

Cusumano, M. A. and D. B. Yoffie (1998), *Competing on Internet Time*, New York: Touchstone.

Essinger, J. (1987), *ATM Networks: Their organization, security and future*, An examination of automated teller machine networks in the United States, United Kingdom, West Germany and France, Oxford: Elsevier International Bulletins.

—— (1992), *Electronic Payment Systems*, London: Chapman & Hall.

European Central Bank (2000), Payment Systems in the European Union – Addendum Incorporating 1998 Figures, February 2000.

REFERENCES

Fisher, J. C. and R. H. Pry (1971), 'A Simple Substitution Model of Technological Change', *Technological Forecasting and Social Change*, vol. 3, pp. 75–88.

Frazer, F. (1985), 'Personal Computer Software', The Financial Times Media Intelligence Unit.

Gandy, A. (1999), *The Network Bank*, Kent: The Chartered Institute of Bankers.

Garrigan, G. P. (1989), 'Streamlining Payment Systems', Paper given at EFTPOS and Home Services Conference, Sheraton Hotel, Edinburgh, November.

Howells, J. and J. Hine (1991), 'Competitive Strategy and the Implementation of a New Network Technology: The Case of EFTPOS in the UK', *Technology Analysis and Strategic Management*, vol. 3(4), pp. 397–425.

—— (1993), *Innovative Banking: Competition and the management of a new networks technology*, London: Routledge.

Kaplan, J. M. (1995), *Smart Cards: The global information passport*, London: International Thomson Computer Press.

Key Note Market Report: Credit and Other Finance Cards (1999), E. Clarke (ed.), twelfth edn., Middlesex, UK: Key Note Publications Ltd.

Key Note Market Report: Personal Banking (1999), P. Smith (ed.), tenth edn., Middlesex, UK: Key Note Publications Ltd.

Lindsey, I. (1994), *Credit Cards – The authoritative guide to credit and payment cards*, Wiltshire, UK: Rushmere Wynne.

Mandell, L. (1990), *The Credit Card Industry: A history*, Boston, MA: Twayne Publishers.

OECD (1983), *Banking and Electronic Fund Transfers*, Paris: OECD.

O'Hanlon, J. and M. Rocha (1993), *Electronic Banking for Retail Customers*, London: Banking Technology.

Paxson, D. and D. Wood (1998), *Encyclopedic Dictionary of Finance*, Oxford: Blackwell.

Report on the Supply of Credit Card Franchise Services in the United Kingdom (1980), *Credit Card Franchise Services*, London: Her Majesty's Stationery Office.

Retail Management Development Programme (1983), *Banking and Payment Systems*, Brighton, UK: The Retail Management Programme.

REFERENCES

Rothwell, R. (1992), 'Developments Towards the Fifth Generation Model of Innovation', *Technology Analysis & Strategic Management*, vol. 4(1), pp. 73–5.

—— (1992a), 'Successful Industrial Innovation: Critical Success Factors for the 1990s', *R&D Management*, vol. 22(3), pp. 221–39.

Shaw, R. (1991), 'How the Smart Card is Changing Retailing', *Long Range Planning*, vol. 24(1), pp. 111–14.

The Smart Card Forum (1997), *Smart Cards: Seizing strategic business opportunities*, C. A. Allen, W. J. Barr and R. Schultz (eds.), London: Irwin Professional Publishing.

Smith, S. and D. Wield (1988), 'Banking on the New Technology: Cooperation, competition and the clearers', in *New Perspectives on the Financial System*, L. Harris, J. Coakley, M. Croasdale and T. Evans (eds.), London: Croom Helm.

Srivastava, L. and R. Mansell (1998), 'Electronic Cash and the Innovation Process: A User Paradigm', Working Paper No. 35, Science Policy Research Unit, University of Sussex, UK.

Utterback, J. and W. Abernathy (1975), 'A Dynamic Model of Process and Product Innovation', *Omega*, vol. 3(6), pp. 639–56.

Vartanian, T. P., R. H. Ledig and L. Bruneau (1998), *Twenty-First Century Money, Banking & Commerce*, Washington, D.C.: Fried, Frank, Harris, Shriver & Jacobson.

Williamson, J. M. (1981), 'Pricing Money Transfer Services', *Journal of Bank Research*, vol. 11, pp. 227–32.

Woodman, B. (1988), 'EFTPOS Who pays? Who benefits?', *Banking World*, June, pp. 46–9.

Woodman, R. C. and A. J. Diver (1988), *EFTPOS – Who Pays? Who Benefits?*, London: Retail Consortium.

Worthington, S. (1992), 'Plastic Cards and Consumer Credit', *International Journal of Retail & Distribution Management*, vol. 20(7), pp. 3–9.

—— (1996), 'The Cashless Society', in *Payments: Past, present and future*, London: Association for Payment Clearing Services.

Index

Abbey National, 3–5, 9–10, 41, 59
Access Card, 23, 26–8, 33–4, 46, 60
acquirer, 7, 14, 24–5, 28, 35, 41, 48, 53–4, 61, 89
American Express, 10, 22–3, 27, 30, 69, 97–9, 101, 106
APR rates, 34, 36
ATM/cash card innovation, vi, viii, 1–20, 40, 43, 46, 53–61, 72, 76–9, 83–9, 107, 110, 114

Banco Santander, 11
BankAmericard, 22–3
Barclaycard, 26–37, 41, 60, 71–5, 82
BarclayCash, 3, 5, 18, 60, 73, 75
Base 24 software/system, 7, 42
BASE-I, 24
benefits
   expected benefits, 71
   external benefits, 18, 53, 59, 71–3
   internal benefits, 32, 53, 62, 71, 110
Big Four, 11, 14, 16, 28, 32, 48, 61, 67
   Four banks/ Four banks network, 2, 8–10, 16–7, 46, 59, 61, 67, 73
Biometrics, 77
BIS (Business Inaugural Service), 39
Blue Card, 98
Boots/ Boots Advantage Loyalty Card, 96–7, 105
BT Cellnet, 31, 34, 71, 74
Building Societies Act, 2, 7, 17, 19

Cardcash, 3, 5, 18, 60, 73
Cashpoint, 3, 5, 60, 73
CEPS (Common Electronic Purse Specifications), 82, 90
chip/ chip card technology, viii, 76, 80–3, 87–9, 94, 97–8, 100–1

Cirrus, vi, 2, 4, 59–60
co-branded credit card, 23, 96–7
collaboration, 2–3, 14, 17, 19–20, 31, 38, 45, 55, 57, 59–60, 71–8, 106, 109, 114
   collaborative strategy, 17–8, 71–3
   horizontal collaboration, 74–5
   vertical collaboration, 74–5
Committee of London Clearing Banks (CLCB), 39, 41
competition, 2, 14, 19–20, 28, 30, 33–8, 46–8, 53, 55, 60–1, 71, 73–4, 90, 93, 99, 103, 108–14
competitive advantage, vii, 17–20, 33–6, 54, 61, 72–3, 75, 108
competitive strategy, 17, 53, 56, 72, 109
Connect card, 46, 53
contact, 84, 100
   contactless technology, 84, 98
   contactless integrated circuit cards, 84
Counterplus, 40–1, 47
credit cards, vi, viii, 1, 21–38, 43, 46, 53, 55–7, 60–2, 72–81, 96, 112, 114
   auto makers, 30
cross-sell, 18, 32, 54, 56
customer hold, 61–2, 72, 99

De La Rue, 3, 5
demand pull, 58, 107
debit cards see EFTPOS/ debit card innovation
DES (Data Encryption Standard), 7, 45
diffusion, 14, 39, 48, 50, 59, 72, 77, 80, 110, 112, 114
digital certificates, 77, 90
Diners/ Diners club, 10, 22–3, 27, 30, 60
dual acquirer/ duality/ duality system, 41, 48, 74

EEPROM (Electrically Erasable Programmable Read Only Memory), 83

EFTPOS
debit card innovation, vi–viii, 38–57, 60–2, 72–5, 77, 114
network/ system/ terminals, vii, 39–47, 53–6, 58, 60, 86, 110

Egg Card, 23, 30–1, 52, 96–7

electronic cash (e-cash), 80–1, 85–7, 90, 99, 101–2, 106

electronic commerce (e-commerce), 52, 90, 102

EMV (Europay, MasterCard, Visa), 86–90, 109

encryption algorithm, 7, 39–40, 78

Enfield, 5

EPROM (Erasable Programmable Read Only Memory), 83

ETAN, 42

Eurocard, 27, 34

Europay, 11, 85–6, 90, 109

financial innovations, vi–vii

Four banks/ Four banks network *see* Big Four

Global IP Mobility strategy, 92

Global System for Mobile Communications (GSM), 86, 95, 105

Guelph, 85, 107

Halifax, 2–5, 9–10, 18, 41, 46, 60, 73

honour-all-cards rule, 46, 56

INET (Interbank Network for Electronic Transfer), 24

innovation management, viii, 72

integrated network, 73

interchange fees, 11, 14, 18–9, 25

International Air Transport Association (IATA), 25

International Organisation of Standards (ISO), 6, 25, 80, 82, 84, 100

internet card, 30–1

interoperability, 55, 85, 87, 111, 113

issuer, 2, 6–7, 14, 25, 28, 30–6, 42–3, 48, 56–61, 71, 99, 106–13

Joint Credit Card Company (JCCC), 23, 26–7

LINK, 2–5, 9–11, 17, 46–7, 59–60, 72–3

Lloyds, 2–12, 14, 17–8, 26, 29, 31–4, 41, 45–8, 51, 59–60, 73

loyalty cards, 30, 81, 93, 96–7

Maestro, 41, 52, 56, 60

magnetic stripe/ magnetic stripe card/ magnetic stripe technology, 4–6, 24–5, 76–9, 86–7

MAOSCO, 82, 111

market pull *see* demand pull

MasterCard, 1–4, 11, 22–4, 27–9, 33–6, 41, 46, 48, 52, 59–60, 72–3, 82–90, 109–10, 113–14

Matrix, 2, 4, 9, 17, 60

merchant (retailer), 25–8, 33, 35–6, 41, 46, 48, 53–5, 84–5, 89, 99, 113

Merchant Service Charge (MSC), 25

Microsoft, 82, 87, 106, 109–10, 113–14

Midland, 2–5, 8–12, 14, 17, 26, 28, 82, 34, 40–1, 45, 47–8, 51–5, 59–60, 82, 85

Mint, 2, 4, 8–10, 17, 46, 59–60, 73

mobile banking, 31, 34, 36, 71, 74, 92

mobile commerce (m-commerce), 82, 92, 94

Mondex system, 82, 85–7, 102, 108–14

multi-application, 86, 90, 106, 112–13

Multos (Multipurpose operating system), 82, 86–7, 109–11, 113

NatWest, 2–8, 12, 14, 17, 23, 26, 29–34, 40–1, 45, 47–8, 51–5, 59, 74

NCR, 5, 7

networking, 1–11, 14, 17–21, 24, 26–8, 32–6, 38, 41–8, 52–60, 72–3, 76, 78, 86, 92–3, 98–9, 108–12

non-banks/ non-financial institutions, 18, 21, 30, 81–2

Octopus, 98, 100

Office of Fair Trading (OFT), 48

off-line systems, 5–7, 18, 78

on-line/ on-line systems, 7, 23, 38, 41, 52, 84, 96, 98

on-line credit card services, 23

open network/ open technology, 17, 59, 86

Open Platform, 82, 86–7, 109–11, 113

open system, 20, 34, 36, 48, 54–5, 72–4, 86

pay TV service, 81, 91, 102

PDQ, 39, 41, 43, 47
Personal Identification Number (PIN),
    vi, 1–3, 6–7, 38, 41, 45, 47, 78, 88–9
Plus (Visa Plus), vi, 1–2, 4, 59–60
POS/EFTPOS, vi–viii, 38–58, 60–2,
    72–5, 77, 86, 110, *see also*
    EFTPOS/debit card innovation
PROM (Programmable Read Only
    Memory), 80, 83
proprietary networks, 1–7, 9, 11, 14,
    17–9, 53, 56, 59, 73
Proton/ Proton Card/ Proton World,
    82, 87, 109–11, 114

revolving credit, 22, 35
Rothwell, 57–8
RSA, 39, 43, 45

scale economies, 28, 30, 46
SET (Secure Electronic Transaction)
    standard, 82, 90
Shell Smart, 96–7, 106
SIM card, 80, 86, 94
smart cards, vi, viii, 76–114
Smart Card Centre of Excellence, 97–8
Solo, 52
Speedline, 40–1
Standard Committee, 17, 84
strategy, vii–viii, 2, 14, 17–9, 32–6, 52–6,
    71–5, 92, 97–9, 109

Streamline, 40–1, 47
supermarket banking, 23, 30
Swindon, 82, 85
Switch
    operator/ technology, 6–7, 24, 41
    cards, 45–6, 48–50, 52–5, 60, 72
    fees, 11, 14, 19
Systems Integration and Networking
    (SIN) model, 57–8

Technical Committee, 68, 84
Technology Push, 19, 57–8, 106
transport cards, 80–1, 87, 91, 98–100
Travel and Entertainment (T&E) card,
    22–3

UKII, 26
Unified Debit Card Scheme (UDCS), 41,
    45

Visa, 1–4, 22–4, 28–9, 33–6, 43–9, 53,
    59–60, 82–92, 107–14
    Cash, 85–7
    Debit/ Visa Delta, 41, 46, 49–50, 53–5
    Visa Electron, 52

Wireless Application Protocol (WAP),
    92, 94
Windows for Smart Cards, 87, 108–10